D1172893

ZION
RECONSIDERED

When the Lord restored the fortunes of Zion,
We were like those who dream.

(Psalm 126:1.)

Yea, He saith:
"It is too light a thing that thou shouldest be My servant
Merely to raise up the tribes of Jacob,
And to restore the preserved ones of Israel.
I will also give thee for a light unto the nations,
That My salvation may reach unto the end of the earth."

(Isaiah 49:6.)

Your own eyes shall see this,
And ye shall say:
"Great is the Lord,
Beyond the border of Israel."

(Malachi 1:5.)

ZION
RECONSIDERED

by
Jakob J. Petuchowski

TWAYNE PUBLISHERS, INC.
New York

Contents

Introduction 7

Chapter One: The Nation That Dwells in Zion 14

Chapter Two: Philanthropy—and Politics 49

Chapter Three: The Spiritual Center 67

Chapter Four: Challenge to American Judaism 88

Chapter Five: "Life Insurance" Against Anti-Semitism? 110

Chapter Six: Once More "The Mission of Israel" 117

Glossary 134

Suggestions For Further Reading 138

Index 141

Introduction

The history of Judaism is a history in which periods of stability and inertia alternate with epochs of revolutionary change. It is the genius of Judaism that it has always understood the need to preserve the dynamics of change even during periods of stability, and to confront revolutionary disruptions with a confidence born of deep roots in tradition. This, however, is not to say that, while the changes themselves are occurring, there are not momentary disturbances of the equilibrium, periods of vacillation and indecision, of temporary imbalance and sudden confusion. It always takes some time for the equilibrium to be re-established. The revolutionary change must first be lived through completely, fully experienced, digested and understood. Only then can it be properly evaluated, reacted to, and, in turn, affect the future course of life and thought.

Such, for example, was the state of affairs in the sixth century B.C.E., when the Kingdom of Judah was destroyed by the Babylonians, and its people led into exile. The first reaction was one of utter despair. "How can we sing the song of the Lord on alien soil?!" (Psalm 137: 4.) The faith of Israel had been bound up so completely with Palestinian life and the Jerusalem sanctuary that removal from that soil, and inability to continue the ancestral sacrificial cult, seemed to spell spiritual and religious death. Gradually, however, the people found themselves singing the song

8   ZION RECONSIDERED

of the Lord on Babylonian soil, and the Prophets, arising
in their midst, men like Ezekiel and Deutero-Isaiah, were
actually able to deepen the faith and to widen its scope,
preaching the doctrine of individual responsibility, and
making the worship of Israel's God available to all of
mankind.

A similar crisis confronted the Rabbis in the year 70
C.E. when the Romans, crushing the Jewish patriot rebellion, put an end to the last vestiges of Jewish national
independence, and set the torch to the Temple on Moriah's
heights. Again, there were those in Israel who felt that their
whole world had come to an end. There were those who
abstained from meat and from wine, seeing that sacrifices
and libations could no longer be offered up on the Lord's
altar. Teachers like Rabbi Yohanan ben Zakkai, long convinced that Judaism's survival depended more on religious
learning and practice than on the accouterments of state-
hood, fought this tendency, and weaned their disciples from
an asceticism born of despair. More than this, they taught
that Torah study, prayer, and deeds of loving-kindness
were adequate substitutes for the priestly cult; and they
distinguished between those parts of Revelation which had
applicability to Temple and State, and those many remaining parts which addressed the Jew wherever he may be.
Thus was a foundation laid which enabled Rabbinic Judaism
to survive and to flourish in many a center of Jewish
life far away from the ancestral Homeland.

A revolutionary change of a different kind affected Jewish life as a result of the ideas which inspired the American
and the French Revolutions. Long treated as an outcast
in Christian society, the Jew, at last, was also to benefit
from the recognition of the Rights of Man. The Ghetto
walls fell. Emancipation came to the Jew in the West.
And Judaism was faced with an unprecedented situation.
Some of the rabbis of the old school did not hesitate to
oppose this change for the better in the status of the Jew.

They were afraid that contact with the language and the culture of the Gentile world would seduce the Jews into apostasy and unfaithfulness to their tradition. Almost as if to substantiate those fears, there were many among the first generation of emancipated Jews who jettisoned their faith and their piety together with the externals of enforced Ghetto existence, many whose devotion to the dominant culture brought with it a conversion to the dominant faith. It was indeed a period of crisis in Jewish life. But Judaism was to master it. Reform Judaism, Conservative Judaism, and Modern Orthodoxy came into being, all of them, in spite of their differing emphases, combining loyalty to the ancestral faith with attachment to the cultural values of the West. Thus was Judaism equipped to meet the spiritual needs of those born and raised in an atmosphere of freedom, where Judaism became a matter of voluntary affiliation, and not one of external compulsion.

And then came the changes, the catastrophes, and the crises of the middle of the twentieth century, the revolutions which we have witnessed within our own lifetime. First, there was the destruction of European Jewry, the murder of the six million. This catastrophe has raised questions about the future of Jewish learning, since the great European centers used to constitute the reservoir of Jewish scholarship. It has shaken many people's faith in human progress, in the depth of Western man's adherence to his supposed values. Even more serious, it has brought into focus again the age-old problem of theodicy, of "justifying God's ways to men." The old response to the effect that we are suffering "on account of our sins" is felt to be woefully inadequate. Instead, more than ever before, Jews are grappling with problems of the goodness of God, of His omnipotence, and even of His very existence.

Jews are still grappling. The answers are not yet in sight. The terrible event itself has not yet been sufficiently "digested" for it to be relegated to a mere niche within an

intelligible Jewish scheme of things. One of the tentative
"explanations," that the slaughter of European Jews was
necessary in order to prepare mankind's conscience for the
establishment of the State of Israel, seems to be as woefully
inadequate as the more traditional response of "on account
of our sins."

But the State of Israel has come into existence; and its
coming into existence constitutes the second great revolution in Jewish life to which we ourselves have been wit-
nesses. It, too, demands a response in terms of the accumulated Jewish tradition of some four millennia. It, too, forces
us to do some serious rethinking of inherited notions. It
calls for a reappraisal of one's concept of the Jewish future
and destiny.

Israel, to those who have witnessed her birth and her
phenomenal progress, is an exhilarating—not to say, intoxi-
cating—experience. It is certainly no less exciting and exhilarating than was the fall of the Ghetto walls to the first generation of the Emancipation. And the reactions, so far, have
suffered from the same lack of balance and equilibrium. The
old messianic dream, in its most literal sense, seems to be on
the verge of realization. After two thousand years, an
independent Jewish State has again arisen on Palestinian
soil. The attacks of numerically superior invaders have
been successfully repulsed. The "exiles" are being "gathered
in." "Prophecy" is being "fulfilled." This is one reading
of the facts.

Another reading of the same facts would see in them
the verification of religious and of secular theories of Jewish nationalism which were expounded in the nineteenth
century—theories which, at the time, met with unequivocal
rejection on the part of Orthodox and Reformers alike. The
axioms and the theorems of Jewish nationalism, or Zionism,
seem to have received their final validation by the verdict
of history. They are no longer a subject of debate. They
must no longer be questioned. They represent the only

possible reading of the facts of Jewish history. Or so, at
least, have been the reactions of the vocal majority of
Jews since the State of Israel came into existence in 1948.

Such reactions, it goes without saying, have, for the most
part, been of a purely emotional nature. The confrontation
of the State of Israel with the totality of the Jewish religious
tradition, and the confrontation of the totality of the Jewish
religious tradition with the fact of the State of Israel, have
not yet taken place. This fact, too, has not yet been sufficiently "digested." It may, moreover, very well be that the
wounds inflicted by the European holocaust but twenty
years ago do not allow us to view the realities of the State
of Israel with the kind of objectivity and detachment which
Judaism's coming to terms with this latest revolution in
Jewish life demands.

But a start has to be made somewhere. Jews who so
recently have been the victims of nationalist emotionalism
run wild in Europe should be the last to wallow in an
aura of nationalist self-satisfaction which permits of no
rational analysis of the true state of affairs. Sooner or later
—and it had better be sooner—they will have to see the
fraction of Jewish existence, which is the State of Israel,
in the perspective of the totality of Jewish existence, an
existence which has never refused to relate to revolutions
and to crises with a willingness to adjust and with a God-
given right to judge.

The following pages are meant to be such a start. They
are not a travel guide to Israel, though the author has
been greatly impressed by Israel's "Biblical landscape."
They are not an analysis of the "welfare state" under Jewish
auspices, though the author has had occasion to be impressed both favorably and unfavorably by the way that
young country has been handling the problems of human
relations. They are not an attempt to theorize about the
psychology of Israel's citizens, though the author has
found among them both extreme kindness and base chican-

ery, gracious hospitality and unpleasant arrogance. They are not, finally, a call for a change in Israel's status quo in the religious sphere, though, as an ordained Reform rabbi, the author might have ample cause for raising such a call. In fact, this book is not so much about the State of Israel itself as it is about those theories and assertions which Jews, particularly in the United States, have come to accept uncritically on the strength of the State of Israel's mere existence. The book, in short, represents a testing of Zionist pronouncements by the touchstone of Israeli realities. Long immersed in the study of contemporary philosophies of Jewish life, and of their relation to the classical sources of Judaism, the author was able to supplement his theoretical knowledge by the concrete experience of a whole year spent in Israel's capital.

If the following pages contain criticism, such criticism is less of the State of Israel—a friendly country—than it is of the attempts, made on that country's behalf, to influence the whole structure of Jewish life in the United States. If the political uses to which philanthropy is being put are exposed in this book, it is because the author would like to see philanthropy freed from political control, and not because of any opposition to the philanthropic support of those Israeli Jews who are in need of such support. On the contrary, the support of fellow Jews, wherever they live, is an important component of the author's whole religious orientation; and, in his view, American Jews have a definite obligation toward the rehabilitation of those of their persecuted brethren who have found a refuge in the State of Israel. Similarly, the criticism of the political manipulation of the channels of Jewish education in America is a criticism made within the context of an absolute commitment to maximum standards in Jewish education and Hebraic learning. It is not the channels and institutions of Jewish education that are the object of criticism here, but the uses to which those institutions are being put in the furtherance of a political aim. It is within the framework of Jewish affirmation that this book undertakes a reconsideration of current Zionist dogma and endeavor.

As such, it is hoped, the book will give impetus to some much needed discussion, and to the laying of the foundations of a healthier relationship between the Jewish citizens of the State of Israel and the wider brotherhood of Jews in the so-called Diaspora.

CHAPTER ONE

The Nation That Dwells in Zion

"We consider ourselves no longer a nation, but a religious community." Thus spoke the Reformers gathered in Pittsburgh, Pennsylvania, in 1885. Their statement was no great innovation. Similar declarations had already been made by Jews in France and in Germany. Like sentiments had been voiced wherever Jews had been permitted to leave the confining walls of the Ghetto, and to partake of the fruits of Emancipation. Nor was this rejection of Jewish nationhood confined to the circles of the Reformers. When modern Jewish nationalism appeared on the scene, its reception on the part of the Orthodox—whether of the East European type or of the Westernized variety—was not in the least any more cordial than the welcome it received on the part of the Reformers. To this day, when stripped of its mythological and ritualistic overtones, the opposition of the Jerusalem *Natoré Kartha* to the State of Israel is engendered by an ideology not too different from that espoused by the American Council for Judaism.

Yet both of these groups are now considered to be extremist "fringe groups," bypassed by the developments of history. Possession is nine-tenths of the law, and the "Jewish Nation" is in possession of its ancestral soil, or, at least, of parts of it. The Jewish state is a *fait accompli*. Ideological opposition to its existence is frowned upon by large segments of American Jewry whose attachment to

14

their Jewish background has been so completely denuded of religious meaning that identification with the people of Zion provides, for many of them, the sole expression of their Jewishness. History has triumphed over ideology.

History has triumphed—both in achievement and in tragedy. If Central and Western Europe was the cradle where the dream of full Emancipation was first dreamed in the eighteenth century, it was also the birthplace of an ideology which, translated into diabolic practice in the twentieth century, led to the murder of some six million Jews. There was a rude and horrible awakening from the dream of Emancipation, from the vision of the Jew as a full member of Western society and participant in its culture.

The image of the "German of the Jewish faith" had been dealt a shattering blow, and Jews elsewhere began to doubt the image of the Frenchman, or the Englishman, or even the American of the Jewish faith. If German Jews were persecuted as "Jews," irrespective of their religious attachment or lack thereof, then, so it was, and is being, argued, the Jews cannot be a mere religious community. They must be a nation, fundamentally different from their "host-peoples." As a nation, they need a homeland of their own. And this proposition has succeeded in winning the assent of thousands of Jews who do not have the slightest intention of immigrating into the Jewish Homeland, now that it exists.

History has triumphed. The modern Jew smiles at the theories and the platforms of the era of Emancipation. The "Jewish" traffic light in Jerusalem shines brighter than the messianic hope of the Pittsburgh Reformers. The Jewish policeman on Tel-Aviv's Dizengoff Square is a more concrete symbol of reality than the rabbi who, together with Protestant and Catholic clergymen, participates in the inauguration ceremonies of the American President.

But over what has history really triumphed? And how soon after the event is the lesson of history clearly discernible? Mention has already been made, in the Introduction,

of the Babylonian conquest of the Kingdom of Judah, in
the sixth century B.C.E., i.e., before the Common Era. The
Babylonians saw in their victory a clear proof of the superiority of the Babylonian gods over the God of the Jews.
The Jews discerned different lessons in this event. They
learned to appreciate the Prophetic insight that a victory
over a sinful Israel can still be a victory of the God of
Israel, whose moral demands are so absolute that even the
fact of "chosenness" is no excuse for moral dereliction.

They learned more. From despair at their inability to "sing
the song of the Lord on alien soil" they progressed to the
recognition that, unlike the gods of other peoples, the God
of Israel is not geographically and territorially bound. The
song of the Lord *could* be sung on alien soil. His teachings
could be studied and practiced far away from Zion. And
when Cyrus gave his permission to the exiles to return to
Judaea, only a fraction of them availed themselves of it.
We do not know too much about Jewish life in Babylonia
at that period. But we do know that, when spirits were low
in the reconstituted Jewish commonwealth, material and
religious help was forthcoming from the Jewish community
in Babylonia—just as some five centuries later it was Hillel
the Babylonian who helped lay the foundations of Rabbinic
Judaism in Palestine.

On the other hand, the followers of Jesus of Nazareth in
the first century, the followers of Sabbatai Zevi in the
seventeenth century, and some of the Jewish Reformers in
the nineteenth century, all committed the same mistake.
They did not allow enough time to elapse in order to gain
perspective. They read the signs of history too soon, and
suffered from illusions of messianic fulfilment when, in fact,
the world was as yet unredeemed. The lesson they bequeath
to us is the danger of jumping to conclusions on the basis
of historical events while they are as yet in progress. The
Messiah did not answer to the name of Napoleon or of
Bismarck. We know that now. They might not have been

able to know it then. But it does not follow from their mistaken identification that the Messiah answered to the name of Theodor Herzl. This, too, could turn out to be a case of mistaken identification.

Nor does the temporary victory, with all of its terrible consequences, of German National Socialism prove that the early Reformers were altogether wrong in their aspirations. It does not even prove that the Jews are a foreign nation in countries other than Palestine, or a "nation at home" on Palestinian soil. Such a reaction to events in recent history, moreover, is possible only when the presuppositions of the anti-Semitic enemy are accepted. Theodor Herzl, for one, did not hide the fact that he did just that. (See Alex Bein, *Theodore Herzl.* Philadelphia, 1941, pp. 162ff.)

But does the triumph of tragedy in recent Jewish history really set at nought the proposition that Jews "are no longer a nation, but a religious community"? Since when have Jews, of all people, let the hard facts of tragic history upset their most deeply cherished convictions? They did not do it, as we have already seen, when the First Temple was destroyed. They did not do it when the Second Temple met with a like fate. The numerical superiority of paganism in antiquity, and of Christianity and Islam in the Middle Ages, never made the Jew doubt that the truth was in his possession, and has remained unsuperseded. His remained the conviction that Jewish destiny was decided "not by might, and not by power, but by My spirit, saith the Lord." (Zechariah 4: 6.)

Yet the joint and related phenomena of modern anti-Semitism and modern Jewish nationalism were to have quite a different repercussion on the outlook and self-consciousness of modern Judaism. Within the span of one lifetime, both Orthodox and Reform Judaism have given in to the twin pressures of anti-Semitism and Zionism. Conservative Judaism, from its very inception in America, had always been more favorably disposed toward some of the basic

Zionist assumptions and the Zionist stress on Jewish "people-hood." This, however, did not prevent its leading spokes-man, Solomon Schechter, from speaking out against "the brutal Torah-less nationalism promulgated in certain quar-ters." (Solomon Schechter, *Some Aspects of Rabbinic Theology*. London, 1909, p. 105.) But by now, as has already been noted, only the Orthodox *Natoré Kartha* and the American Council for Judaism vocally maintain the tradi-tional objection to the secularization of Jewish loyalties.

There is, of course, no denying of the fact that, in an-tiquity, there was such a thing as a Jewish nation, even though modern definitions of nationhood would hardly be applicable in all respects. The intertwining of religion and nationality was such that conversion to the Jewish religion implied acceptance of Jewish peoplehood, while religious apostasy *ipso facto* entailed exclusion from the body politic. After the final destruction of the Jewish State, in the year 70 C.E., i.e., of the Common Era, the spiritual leaders of the people did indeed distinguish between those parts of the divine law which were bound up with possession of a national territory and those parts which retained their valid-ity wherever Jews lived. But a sharp distinction between religion and nationality was still not made; and this for two reasons: in the first place, the nuances of the modern defini-tions were not then available. Secondly, and perhaps of even greater importance, both in the Christian Roman Empire and in Parthian Babylonia, the Jews, on account of their religious peculiarities, stood outside of society, and, in large measure, were granted sufficient autonomy to conduct their internal affairs in accordance with their own traditional laws. The same applied, later on, to the Jewish communi-ties under Muslim rule, in spite of the considerable amount of participation they were allowed in the conduct of the affairs of state and in the shaping of the general culture.

It applied even more to the later centuries of Christian domination, when the Jews were ever more strictly excluded from the body politic, until even their residence was legally restricted to the narrow lanes of the Ghetto. There can be no doubt that the self-governing Jewish enclaves within (or rather, without) Christian society considered themselves as Jewish communities "in exile," and the liturgical poetry they produced is evidence of their longing for a return to a messianically redeemed Zion. But it was still true, even in the Ghetto, that there was no concept of Jewish people-hood, let alone nationality, apart from adherence to the Jewish religion. When Saadia Gaon, in the tenth century, said, "our nation is a nation only because of its possession of the Torah," he was giving expression to the only form of Jewish identification known to the pre-Emancipation Jew. By the same token, throughout the Jewish Middle Ages, conversion to Christianity or Islam removed the convert from the Jewish *people*—in practice, if not altogether in theory.

For almost eighteen centuries Jews led this kind of existence. Excluded, on account of their religion, from the society upon whom they were economically dependent, they had every reason to feel like aliens even in territories where they had taken up residence long before the populations which were later to constitute their citizenry. The frequent expulsions of Jews from one territory to another, instigated by the Church *ad majorem gloriam Dei*, only confirmed the feeling of "exile."

Then came the eighteenth century, the Century of Enlightenment. Enlightenment ideas and ideals led to the American and French Revolutions. These, in turn, spread concepts such as the Rights of Man, of Liberty, Equality and Fraternity, and led to the Separation of Church and State. Thus was born the Emancipation of the Jew, of the *Western* Jew, that is to say. For Emancipation did not reach the Jew of Russia until 1917, and the status of the Jew in Muslim lands (though often comparing favorably with that of the Jew under Christian rule) has always been determined by the Koran as being midway between that of the true believer and that of the pagan.

It was the Jew who stepped out of the Ghetto who had to find his bearings. It was he who now brought his civil suits before the civil courts instead of submitting them to the rabbinical *beth din*. And it was he who, with all of his attachment to the ancestral faith, now felt that linguistically, culturally, and politically, he belonged to the country of his birth. When, therefore, the question was put to him about the meaning of his Jewish identity, he quite naturally answered: "We consider ourselves no longer a nation, but a religious community."

This answer would never have been understood by the Jew in Eastern Europe, for his position had remained unchanged. He was still living in the Middle Ages. Emancipation had not yet come to him. He was not a part of Russian or Polish society. He was thrown on to his own resources, and he created his own Jewish culture, and language, and even cuisine. But, though legal Emancipation did not come to the Jew of the East, the currents of modern thought did not altogether pass him by. Positivism, agnosticism, and even atheism, made vocal and respectable after the demise of the Christian State, found their echoes among the rebellious *yeshivah* students of Eastern Europe, and led to a rejection of the traditional religious heritage, without, at the same time, leading to a conversion to Christianity. Here, now, was nonreligion or antireligion within a Jewish environment. But the environment was still there, and one was part of it. This, too, called for a new definition of one's Jewishness.

It was the Jew of the East who reversed the declaration of the Pittsburgh Reformers. "We consider ourselves no longer a religious community, but a secular nation." The modern nationalist struggles of Greece, of Italy, and of Poland, were to have their counterpart in a Jewish national revival in Palestine.

Secularization brought the Eastern Jew to Zionism. Herzl, the Western Jew, was brought to it by anti-Semitism. His programmatic work, *The Jewish State* (1896), was Herzl's reaction to the Dreyfus *Affaire*. Some fifty years later, the State of Israel came into being. Israel has solved any number of problems, problems of agriculture and construction, problems of strategy and defense, problems of science and industrialization. However, it has not solved "The Jewish Problem." And it has brought into focus a question lurking in the background ever since Emancipation came to the Jew in the West, and secularization to the Jew in the East. It has brought the question into focus. And the question nearly led to the fall of a government. But it has not answered the question—the unanswered question of the Jewish State: Who is a Jew?

The question, "Who is a Jew?" agitated the minds of the Israelis, and had its repercussions in world Jewry, some years ago, when it arose as a simple matter of administrative policy. Israelis are required by law to carry identity cards. One of the particulars entered upon those identity cards is the bearer's religion. Now, in the vast majority of cases this presents no problem. According to traditional Jewish law, a man is a Jew either if his mother was Jewish or if he himself has become converted to Judaism according to the requirements of Rabbinic law. However, in countries other than Israel, the letter of the traditional law has not always been strictly followed. Besides, the Israeli Orthodox authorities—and they are the only "recognized" Jewish religious authorities in the country—refuse a priori to recognize the validity of any case of conversion to Judaism which came about under non-Orthodox auspices. In other words, a person's affirmation of his own Jewishness could be queried by the rabbinate, and, if found unsubstantiated according to the rabbinate's own lights, met with outright rejection.

The short history of the State of Israel has already been marked by a few notorious cases where Jewish marriage rites, and even Jewish burials, have been refused to people whose claim to Jewishness did not stand up to rabbinic scrutiny. The same kind of rigorous following of the letter of the law was now to be applied to the identity cards carried by Israeli citizens. That, at least, was the demand of the rabbinate and of the clericalist political parties.

This *cause célèbre* ended in a kind of draw. The problem was evaded rather than solved. The simple expedient was used of stating on the identity cards of those of mixed descent the religions of both father and mother. Whoever read the identity cards could then draw his own conclusions. But the fact that the problem could arise in the first place is a clear indication that something very basic and fundamental has not yet been properly faced and thought out by the State of Israel. Is the State of Israel a modern secular state? Or is it a "Torah State," a theocracy? As matters stand now, it partakes a little of each. While the State of Israel has thus far postponed the drawing up of a constitution, its Declaration of Independence does guarantee the various freedoms of a modern democracy, including the freedom of religion. At the same time, the religious freedom of the Jew (though not that of the non-Jew) is restricted. By this we do not mean that he is forced to worship according to a certain pattern. He is not. He may refrain from worship altogether, or he may worship in non-Orthodox synagogues. A few of the latter kind have already been established. But in matters of his personal status (i.e., marriage, divorce, etc.) he is subject to the Orthodox Rabbinical Courts, and he has no other recourse. Moreover, non-Orthodox rabbis cannot be "recognized" by the state, as the law stands at the moment.

It has to be pointed out that, legally speaking, this represents no usurpation on the part of the Orthodox. It is, rather, the law of the land as established by a democratically elected parliament and government. True, the majority of the population are *not* Orthodox. But the government is composed of a coalition between Labor and clericalist parties, and concessions to the Orthodox are a part of the current political "deal." The Law of Personal Status is one such concession. The prohibition of pig breeding is another. The laws restricting Sabbath traffic are a third. And the demands of the clericalists are by no means exhausted as yet. Only a complete change in the composition of the government could bring an end to this situation, which is popularly known as the "salami," from which the clericalists cut off slice after slice. At any rate, it has to be admitted that, with all their increasing power, the clericalists do set about turning the State of Israel into a "Torah State" by means which, under present Israeli law, are both democratic and legitimate.

It is, furthermore, not our concern in this chapter to argue for a change in the status quo. Ours is rather an interest in the situation as it obtains at the moment, for this situation clearly demonstrates the dilemma of a nation which, on the one hand, wants to be known as a modern, democratic, and secular nation, and which, on the other hand, lays claim to the traditional Jewish heritage—nay, which claims to be the only legitimate form of Jewish existence.

Theodor Herzl, who did not dream about this particular problem, nevertheless gave expression to its ingredients when he wrote his blueprint of *The Jewish State*. Herzl, it will be remembered, was a "westerner," and, when he wrote *The Jewish State*, he had not yet been in contact with the East European Jewish masses. Herzl was a "westerner" who saw in Jewish nationalism, and in the acquisition of a Jewish homeland, the answer to anti-Semitism, and the solution to the "Jewish Problem." But the national movement was something to be created anew, as far as Herzl was concerned. It did not yet exist—at least not within the circles with whom Herzl was most familiar. For Herzl, the theoretician of secular Zionism in the West, the Jew was not a Jew on account of any common national culture or national language. On the contrary, the author of *The Jewish State* wrote, "It is only by the faith of our fathers that we recognize our historic community, for we have long since indelibly absorbed the languages of the various nations."

Here, then, was Herzl, dreaming about a Jewish nation and a Jewish State, and yet knowing only too well that the human material he would have to recruit for his project, the "Jews," were a cohesive group, a cohesive *Jewish* group, only because they were able to recognize their historic community by the faith of their fathers. Herzl, in other words, with all of his secularist aims, basically accepted the *religious* definition of the Jew! (This important fact is not always remembered in modern Zionist circles.)

At the same time, Herzl was clearly a modern secularist. Neither in his *The Jewish State* nor in his utopian novel, *Altneuland,* did he envisage the future Jewish State as a theocracy. "We shall know how to keep our rabbis in their synagogues, and our generals in their barracks," wrote Herzl in *The Jewish State.*

Herzl's grand vision is said to have found its fulfilment in the establishment of the State of Israel in 1948. A new edition of *Altneuland* has been published in Israel, showing with ample illustrations in color photography how Herzl's vision has come true. What this new edition of *Altneuland* does not show, however, is that, on the one hand, many of the founders of the State of Israel did *not* recognize their historic community only "by the faith of our fathers," and that, on the other hand, the citizens of the State of Israel did *not* know how to keep their "rabbis in their synagogues." Herzl's vision may have come true; but not without turning upside down two of his basic presuppositions. And that is why, to this day, the question, "Who is a Jew?" has not found its answer in the State of Israel.

So far we have been concerned with the implications of

the question, "Who is a Jew?" more or less within the framework of the problem as it came to the fore in a nexus of political and religious considerations in the State of Israel. There is, however, yet another aspect to this question.

For some time now it has been customary for sociologists studying the Israeli scene to speak of "the two Israels." The reference here is to the two parts of the world whence Israel's present-day population has been primarily recruited —Europe and the Orient. Technically, these two areas of origin of the Israeli population do not necessarily coincide with geographical boundaries. Among Israel's so-called Oriental Jews are to be found also those emanating from North Africa. In common Israeli parlance, one distinguishes between the Ashkenazim and the Sepharadim. Originally, the former term denoted those Jews who used the traditional Jewish liturgy as it had become standardized among the German and Polish Jews, whereas the latter term was applied to Jews following the Spanish and Portuguese rite of the Jewish liturgy. Since Jews of this second category were to be found all around the Mediterranean shore, as well as in Iran and Iraq, and points further east, it would be a mistake to let one's acquaintance with the Spanish and Portuguese Synagogue in Amsterdam, with Bevis Marks in London, or with Shearith Israel in New York, determine his view of the Sepharadim. On the contrary, whereas in the Western world the Sepharadi Jews represented a kind of intellectual and financial aristocracy, the Sepharadim in Israel, by and large, comprise the socially and intellectually inferior strata of society. This, of course, is not meant as a value judgment. Israel's Sepharadim merely reflect the cultural background of the countries whence they have come. Israel offers them—on a long-term basis—the chance of self-improvement.

Israel's Sepharadim feel discriminated against in Israeli society, and they voice many of the complaints vociferously made within recent years by the American Negro. Indeed,

Israel's Sepharadim have become so ethnically self-conscious that, in some local political elections, Sepharadim *qua* Sepharadim have entered the lists—in addition to the more conventional political parties. Whether actual discrimination against the Sepharadim does exist is a question which need not detain us here. It certainly does not exist in any legally sanctioned sense. But the fact remains that, in spite of their ever increasing numbers, the Sepharadim in Israeli society do not belong to the "in-group." A Sepharadi girl is more likely to be employed as a charwoman than as a high-ranking civil servant. The top army "brass" is more likely to be recruited from the ranks of the Ashkenazim, whereas the humble (or not so humble) traffic cop is bound to be a Sepharadi. There is, furthermore, no denying of the fact that, in a number of public schools, Ashkenazi parents are seriously worried by the influx of Sepharadi children, while, at the same time, Sepharadi parents are constantly complaining about their children's lack of equal opportunity in the field of education. If, in the light of all this, one considers that, between May 15, 1948, and December 31, 1961, 466,812 immigrants came to Israel from the Ashkenazi orbit, while 529,078 came from the Sepharadi regions (*Statistical Abstract of Israel* No. 14, Israel Government Central Bureau of Statistics, 1963, page 110), a striking picture is obtained of what the sociologists have in mind when they speak of "the two Israels."

But the phrase is misleading. It creates the impression that the Ashkenazim in Israel represent a unified group, emanating from a common cultural background. This is far from being the case. The Ashkenazi Jew who, hailing from the ghettos of Eastern Europe, has found his new home in the self-imposed ghetto of Jerusalem's Meah She'arim quarter is most unlikely to have shared a common cultural and educational background with the German-Jewish intellectual, turned Marxist, who cultivates the soil of the Esdraelon Valley, and lives in a collective settlement. Nor, for that matter, can all the Russian, Polish, Galician, Hungarian, and Rumanian Jews be lumped together—or any one group of them with the German Jews. The differences in cultural background are so striking that Israelis themselves (or those few of them who are gifted with a sense of humor) are liable to remark on the following: in Hungary, a man will be pointed out as a Jew; in Poland, a man will be pointed out as a Jew; and in Rumania, a man will be pointed out as a Jew. But, when these three Jews come to Israel, the first will be pointed out as a Hungarian, the second as a Pole, and the third as a Rumanian!

There are, then, more than "two Israels." There are any number of them. And each "Israel" is very conscious of being discriminated against, or crowded out, by the next. Still, the majority of the Ashkenazi population is of Polish and Russian antecedents. They form the backbone of the dominating *Mapai* (Labor) Party. The *Mapai* Party is the senior partner of the coalition government, with the result that the key positions in government and civil service are in the hands of those who have received their political schooling in Eastern Europe. At the same time, the Kafkaesque *pakid* (lower-echelon civil servant) with whom the citizen has his most direct contacts is more often than not a member of one of the Oriental communities. The whole thing, in combination, creates something of the atmosphere of Byzantine administration. This may be quite in the tradition of government as Palestinian soil has known it for a very long time. But it does make the German Jew feel that his own temperament and talents are not sufficiently utilized in making of the State of Israel the kind of modern and enlightened commonwealth which Herzl must have had in mind.

Yet the political parties favored by the German immigrants—the Progressives and the General Zionists (which, together, make up the Liberals)—did not gain more than 17 per cent of the total votes cast at the 1961 parliamentary election. (*Statistical Abstract of Israel* No. 14, 1963, page 695.) There are obviously not enough of them in the country to have a greater impact upon the development of things. And there are even fewer "Anglo-Saxons," i.e., Jewish immigrants from English-speaking countries. While Mr. David Ben-Gurion was Prime Minister he addressed frequent calls to the Jews in the West to come to Israel in large numbers. Mr. Ben-Gurion, a *Mapai* man himself, was hardly worried by the preponderance of East European elements. But he was very conscious of the increasing numbers of Sepharadi Jews from underdeveloped countries, and he was looking for the restoration of some kind of balance.

Poles and Algerians, Russians and Syrians, Rumanians and Iraqis, Austrians and Moroccans, Czechs and Kurdistanis, Germans and Indians, Lithuanians and Egyptians, Bulgarians and Yemenis—they all and many more make up the citizenry of the State of Israel, the "Jewish nation" in its Homeland. Or, at least, they are supposed to make it up. It is still a question of "becoming" rather than of "being." There are effective means which help this process along. There is the public school system which labors valiantly to unify the nation, even though the public school system is itself divided into two separate networks, one of which takes Judaism—in its Orthodox variety—very seriously indeed, and one of which does not care for religion at all. There is the army which forces recruits of various ethnic backgrounds to sleep in the same tent and to eat the same food. There is the modernized Hebrew language which promises to become *the* language of the country, and which is already spoken by the young generation born in Israel to the gradual detriment of the knowledge of European languages. And, above all, there are the sealed-off borders surrounding the tiny country, with hostile Arabs arming behind them in anticipation of a "second round," when they hope to drive the Israelis into the sea. All these are factors which make for national strength in Israel.

And what is "Jewish" about all this? "Jewish," in a manner of speaking, is to be on the receiving end of anti-Semitism. Anti-Semitism led Herzl to the formulation of his Zionist philosophy, and the concrete and bloody manifestations of anti-Semitism led masses of Jews to seek refuge on Palestinian soil. But there are many varieties of anti-Semitism, and it may be an over-simplification to regard it as a uniform force, lurking in all countries outside the State of Israel, and dedicated to the destruction of all Jews who do not run to their Homeland in time.

There is a religious anti-Semitism, for many centuries fostered by the Christian Church. Yet that variety, far from wanting to drive the Jew out, rather aimed at drawing him in, at making him a member of Christian society if only he would convert to the dominant faith. Terrible as this form of anti-Semitism was, it can hardly be identified with the Nazi variety of Jew-hatred, which aimed at the physical extermination of all those who, whether Jew, Christian, or atheist, could trace their descent to forebears who were known as Jews—and all this on the basis of a mad and disproved "racial" theory. Yet neither the Christian nor the Nazi form of anti-Semitism has much in common with the disabilities suffered by Jews in certain Communist societies, where Jews are being discriminated against, not because they are Jews, but because, in large numbers, they belong to those economic strata which it is in the interest of the Communist state to liquidate, and because Communism is the sworn foe of any and all religions.

Jewish refugees came to Palestine as victims of all those various forms of anti-Semitism; and this much the different varieties of anti-Semitism do have in common: that, whatever the political, religious, or economic reason which made the existence of a "scapegoat" a necessity, the "scape-

goat" chosen was the Jew! There is, therefore, on the part
of the Jews, a background of common suffering, and, at
the same time, a common desire to survive.

It is classical Zionist doctrine that the only place where
the Jew can escape persecution, and the only place where
he can survive, is the autonomous Jewish State erected upon
the ancestral soil. Yet, upon that very soil, two Jewish
states had already been wiped out—in 586 B.C.E. and in 70
C.E., respectively. Under the circumstances, the Zionist
doctrine must either be understood as a dogmatic assertion
or as a pious hope. In either case, it is not based on historical
precedent, any more than it has given due consideration to
such possible alternatives as are presented, for example,
by British democracy or the "pluralistic society" of the
United States of America.

Even if the Zionist dogma or hope were accepted at face
value, it would still leave us wondering, what is so particularly "Jewish" either about a past clouded by persecution,
or about the desire to survive? Others, in addition to the
Jews, have undergone persecution; and all men have a
desire to survive! We would ask why the State of Israel
should want to be considered as a "Jewish" State, what it
is, in addition to anti-Semitism, that makes it lay claim to
the position of leadership in world Jewry, and to being
the fulfilment of millennial "Jewish" aspirations.

The answer to this question cannot be found in the realm
of culture. Of course, there will be such a thing as an
Israeli culture. It is in the process of being produced at this
very moment. But the mere fact that it is in the process
of coming into being shows that it is not there to begin
with, that it cannot be *the* factor which provides the *initial*
cohesion of the populace. Besides, we have spoken of
"Israeli" culture rather than of "Jewish" culture. "Jewish"
is a far wider concept than "Israeli." There could conceivably be an Israeli culture, just as there is a Rumanian
culture, or an Albanian culture. But for such an Israeli

culture to lay claim to being Jewish culture, it would have
to be something which naturally, and not artificially, grows
out of an uninterrupted Jewish experience of some four
thousand years. Moreover, since the majority of Jews do
not live in the State of Israel, such a culture—if it is to be
"Jewish" rather than merely "Israeli"—would have to be
meaningful to Jews wherever they are, and not just in the
State of Israel.

Yet what people are in the habit of calling "Jewish culture," turns out in the vast majority of cases to be nothing
more than the culture and folkways of a particular Jewish
environment, rather than something universally recognized
by Jews as their cultural heritage. *Blintzes* and *gefillte fish*
come from the East European Jewish cuisine. They were not
part of the culinary culture of the German Jews—not to
speak of the Oriental brethren, whose *falafel* and *humus,* in
their turn, were not part of the fare of European Jews.
(Perhaps the only justification to speak of a Jewish cuisine
at all would be the—at one time—universal observance of
Biblical and Rabbinical dietary laws. But that belongs to
the realm of religion, which will be discussed later.)

When speaking of the higher things in life, much the
same could be said about Jewish music. What passes for
"Jewish music" in many parts of the United States—and in
Israel—is the musical style brought with them by the
masses of East European Jewish emigrants. Again, it is
not particularly identical with the musical tradition of the
Western Jews (compare Yossele Rosenblatt with Darius
Milhaud!), while the music of the Oriental Jew is, to the
untrained Western ear, indistinguishable from the music
of the Arabs. One can, of course, learn to appreciate other
people's musical traditions; but such appreciation does not,
in and by itself, make for a common and shared culture.

Literature could be cited as another instance. Quite
apart from the illiteracy of many of the Oriental Jews,
literature, too, is so very dependent upon the particular

environment whence Jews come that it is impossible to speak of a common "Jewish literature," in which the totality of Jewish life is reflected, and which, in turn, could be certain of the esthetic appreciation of all Jews. (Again, an exception must be made in the case of Biblical and Rabbinical literature. But this, too, belongs to the realm of religion, which will be discussed later.)

Language, naturally, as we have already noted, is a cohesive cultural factor. There is the promise (and already the partial fulfilment) of an Israeli Hebrew literature. But the "Jewishness" of this literature is far from being unproblematical. The problem itself is not new; it is only being complicated by Hebrew as the medium of expression. What makes a book "Jewish"? Is it the fact of the author's being a Jew? If so, do we reckon *Das Kapital* by Karl Marx as part of Jewish literature, or do we forget about Karl Marx, since he was, after all, baptized into Christianity? But, then, by the same token, we should also exclude Heinrich Heine's "Princess Sabbath" and "The Rabbi of Bacharach," since Heine, too, was baptized. On the other hand, if the content of a book determines its inclusion or exclusion, does the affiliation of the author enter into our calculations at all? If contents be our criterion, then *About the Spirit of Hebrew Poetry* by the non-Jew Herder would be part of Jewish literature, while *The Psychopathology of Everyday Life* by the Jew Freud would not.

These questions, as we have said, are not new. They antedate the creation of the State of Israel. In fact, they originated, as did Zionism itself, in the secularization of Jewish life which followed the fall of the Ghetto walls. But, outside the State of Israel, such questions, and the proposed answers, are largely academic. Few writers, moved to produce a piece of literature, consciously sit down to "create Jewish literature." People sit down and write. Let the bibliographers worry about the exact classification of the products of their pens! In Israel, the situation is different.

There, it becomes a patriotic duty to aid the growth of the national literature—of a literature, that is to say, which claims to be not only "Israeli," but "Jewish" as well, and of significance to all Jews.

And the use of Hebrew itself could not possibly serve as a criterion. There are beautiful Hebrew translations available in Israel of Plato's *Dialogues,* of Homer's *Iliad,* and even of Kant's *Kritik der reinen Vernunft.* Such works are obviously not part of Jewish, or even Israeli, literature. But what of an Israeli author who writes in Hebrew about a general subject of human interest, imitating yesterday's European literary fashion?

There can be no doubt that the Hebrew poet H. N. Bialik (d. 1934) contributed to Jewish literature. Steeped in the world of Bible and Talmud, his language was rich in associations, his burden—even during moods of rebellion—had reference to the inherited modes of Jewish thought and Jewish living. But, in modern Israel, though the memory of the late poet laureate is still officially revered, and though a few of his works are still being studied in the schools, Bialik's poetry and prose are no longer deemed to be representative of Israeli writing, or even worthy of imitation. The hero of Israeli literature is no longer the devoted student of Torah, but the pioneer with a gun. The link with past Jewish literature becomes somewhat tenuous.

With all of the official propaganda talk about Israel as the only place where "Jewish culture" (as though the very existence of such a thing were beyond all dispute!) can truly flourish, many Israelis themselves are aware of the fact that such a culture will first have to be created. It is easier to talk about "Jewish culture" in homogeneous Jewish groups. Talk about "Jewish culture" in New York City, and chances are that the shared memories of Jewish life in Minsk, Pinsk, and Plotzk, will enable your listeners to associate something concrete with these words. As for the few Jews of German provenance, who do not share those

particular memories—well, they can be ridiculed as "assimila-
tionists!" But in Israel, where Pole confronts Moroccan,
and where Yemenite rubs shoulders with Rumanian, the
absence of a common "Jewish culture" becomes blatantly
obvious. The "flourishing of Jewish culture in the Homeland," and the "Ingathering of the Exiles" were two of
Zionism's chief aims and objectives. It is one of the ironies
of history that, at the very moment when the "Ingathering"
takes place, the existence of Jewish culture itself turns out
to be so questionable.

It is the realization of this dilemma which is undoubtedly
responsible for the feverish search for common cultural
roots in which Israel is engaged. It accounts for the role
which archaeology plays in the life of the young state, a
role which almost amounts to a religious one. In the ruins
of the remote past, in the foundations of the ancestors'
buildings, and in the remnants of their artifacts, one finds
a common cultural bond for their latter-day descendants.
And, of course, "the Land" in and by itself, is milked for
its very last drop of historical associations—if only it can be
shown (or believed) that "the nation that dwells in Zion"
(a favorite phrase in official Israeli pronouncements) today
is composed of the very people which inhabited this region
in Biblical antiquity, spanning the intervening centuries and
millennia with a blithe silence and a blissful ignorance.

Such a state of mind leads to official and government
encouragement of pilgrimages to supposed holy sites, the
authenticity of which is far from having been established.
The place nowadays called Mount Zion, with its "Tomb of
David" (identified as such by medieval Christian tradition),
is a case in point. But perhaps even more pathetic is the
city of Jerusalem itself. Many lives were lost, and much
hardship was endured, in making the New city of Jerusalem
a part of the State of Israel—and this in spite of the United
Nations decision to have both the Old and the New cities
internationalized. Strategically, the position of Israeli Jeru-

salem is a monstrosity. The city is surrounded on three sides by territory of hostile Arabs, and is connected, on the fourth side, to the rest of the State of Israel by means of a narrow "corridor" of mountainous roads which become impassable in inclement weather. Yet Jerusalem, of all places, had to be chosen as the capital of the State of Israel. Not that Jerusalem is in any way an industrial or economic center of the country. But Jerusalem is—Jerusalem! And, in its search for roots, the State of Israel felt impelled to insist that a Jewish State without Jerusalem as its capital was simply unthinkable. At that, it is the sound of the name, with all of its associations, which is the determining factor, rather than the geographical location. For the Jerusalem of history, the "City of David," is in the hands of the Kingdom of Jordan, whereas Israeli-held Jerusalem had its origin barely a century ago.

It is by means of such historical associations that a link is being sought with the country's ancient history and culture, in order to provide a common cultural basis for the country's present-day inhabitants. Alas, memories alone do not suffice, be they ever so authentic, and the task of creating a new culture abides. So does the problem of seeing in the culture which is in the process of becoming not only an "Israeli" culture, but a "Jewish" culture.

We have stated above, in connection with the problem of "Jewish" literature, that the semantic questions associated with the adjective "Jewish" originated in the secularization of Jewish life which followed the fall of the Ghetto walls. But what has been said about the specific area of literature can be applied to the general concept of "Jewish culture" as such. Until the end of the eighteenth, and the beginning of the nineteenth century, there would have been little doubt about the meaning of "Jewish." Everybody knew that something which was "Jewish" was something that pertained to the Jewish *religion*. For, although the Jews in the four corners of the earth may not have shared a common literature, a common music, a common cuisine, or even a common language for everyday use, they did share a common faith, a common religious literature (Bible and Rabbinica), common prayers, and common religious observances. It might be argued that what Jews had in common was, on account of their shared ancestry and history, more than the ecclesiastical paraphernalia of a religious denomination. But no definition of the term "Jewish" which left the religious aspect out of its consideration would have been recognized as accurate and true.

What, then, is the role of the Jewish religion in the State of Israel—particularly as an aspect of the state's "Jewishness," and as a cohesive cultural factor? The answer, in detail, is complicated. But, in an over-all view, it can be stated that few things in the State of Israel are as divisive, setting citizen against citizen, as is the Jewish religion. We have had occasion to note the sociologists' concept of "the two Israels," and we have found that, from the ethnic and cultural points of view, the phrase about "the two Israels" is an understatement. There are many more. But the concept of "the two Israels" could be most fittingly used in dealing with the religious situation of the country.

Israelis are either "religious" (which, in Israel, means Orthodox), or they are nonreligious (if not actively antireligious). But, since religion in the State of Israel is not left to the conscience of the individual, being, instead, a matter of government and legislative concern, one's adherence (or otherwise) to the dictates of Orthodox Judaism becomes a matter of political acrimony and a constant bone of contention. In addition, religious requirements become "negotiable" political positions. This development is due to the existence of clericalist political parties, which trade their votes on domestic and foreign policy for concessions in the religious sphere, i.e., for the right to enforce religious legislation in ever increasing areas of the national life.

This works on both the national and the local levels. We

have already seen that, nationally, the administration of the laws of personal status is in the hands of the Orthodox Rabbinical Courts. An example of the local level would be the problem of public transportation on the Sabbath. In Jerusalem, the clericalists have succeeded in banning public transportation on the Sabbath altogether. In Tel-Aviv, likewise, one cannot ride a bus on the Sabbath. But, on Sabbath afternoon, one can see the buses maneuvering into position, so that they can take on passengers the moment the Sabbath terminates. In Haifa, on the other hand, public transportation is available on the Sabbath. What this means is that the strongest Orthodox representation in city government exists in Jerusalem, the weakest in Haifa.

Yet it is the unconcealed aim and objective of the clericalist parties to gain enough political power to be able to impose the totality of Orthodox Jewish legislation upon the population as a whole. And the illustration of public transportation which we have chosen is only one of many. If the clericalists had their way completely, they would ban not only public transportation on the Sabbath, but any kind of vehicular traffic whatsoever, just as they would ban the consumption of nonkosher meat and other instances of nonobservance in ritual matters.

One of their achievements is the exemption of Orthodox Jewish girls from the military draft, to which all other Israeli girls are subject. Another is the exemption of *yeshivah* students from the draft. Of course, the exemption of theological students from army duty is known in other countries as well. The situation in Israel differs somewhat, though, in that by no means all, or even a majority, of the *yeshivah* students ever intend to serve as rabbis. In other words, it is their Orthodoxy itself, and their preference of religious over secular institutions of learning, which enables them to get out of military duty, though the latter is mandatory for their non-Orthodox contemporaries.

How this privileged position of the Orthodox strikes the

nonreligious can easily be imagined, as can the reaction of
the nonreligious to the clericalist successes in enforcing
Orthodox legislation. Each new clericalist "success" entails
new hatred for religion on the part of the nonreligious. Yet
neither side alone is strong enough to take the government
into its hands. Under the circumstances, political deals and
trades between the two sides continue, as does the increasing success of the clericalists in writing Orthodox Judaism
into the law of the land. And as does the growing animosity
of nonreligious toward religious Judaism.

Far from serving as a unifying cultural factor, therefore,
religion in Israel leads to an ever more pronounced division
among the population. A striking illustration of what this
means is furnished by the education of the young in the
State of Israel. The government maintains two separate educational networks, one for the Orthodox, and one for the
nonreligious. In the Orthodox schools, the boys have to
cover their heads, and their observance of Sabbath and
dietary laws is insisted upon. The curriculum is heavy on
Biblical and Rabbinic texts. On the other hand, the nonreligious schools have no requirements in matters of religious
observance. The amount of traditional Jewish literature
studied is far less than in the Orthodox schools, though Bible
study does form a significant part of the curriculum. But the
Bible is not studied as a religious text; it is presented as the
national literature of the Hebrew nation. The passages
selected for study are passages of national and historical
interest, rather than those of more specific religious significance.

The fact that the government supports both educational
networks does not, however, mean that a peaceful co-
existence has been achieved on this level. The amount of
money spent on each network, the number of buildings
erected, the size of the respective teaching staffs—all of this
becomes a matter for political bickering and personal
recriminations. Party loyalties are at least as strong in

this realm as they are anywhere else. When the Labor Party recently suggested that it, too, would set up schools with a religious outlook, making it possible for parents to give their children a religious education without having to belong to the clericalist parties, the latter broke out in a mighty uproar. They, and they alone, have the monopoly of educating Israeli children religiously! And let all others keep their hands off!

In this connection, it is interesting to note that the Labor Party should have felt the need to provide religious education. Of course, there are political motives. Most of the new Oriental immigrants owe allegiance to Orthodox Judaism, and want to give their children a religious upbringing. The Labor Party would hate to lose those immigrants' votes. But, perhaps, there is something even deeper.

Some years ago, Israelis woke up to the realization that the total absence of religious instruction in the nonreligious public schools has had the effect of alienating the students completely both from two thousand years of Jewish history, and from a feeling of fellowship with contemporary Jews in the world outside the State of Israel. It was thereupon decided to introduce a new subject into the curriculum of the nonreligious public school system: "Jewish Consciousness." As part of this new subject, Jewish customs and ceremonies were to be studied, and selected Rabbinic and prayer texts were to be read. The new subject of "Jewish Consciousness" has not been found to be successful in achieving the goals for which it was designed. In the first place, to force such a subject on more or less unwilling nonreligious, or even antireligious, teachers was hardly calculated to insure the project's success. Secondly, where the project was put into operation in earnest it led to the presentation of the subject in terms of quaint customs and folkways of the distant past, rather than as an attempt to understand the living faith of the live religious Jew.

It should be noted in passing that Israel has no Sunday

schools or religious schools. The Synagogue in Israel, unlike its counterpart in other countries, serves neither as a communal center nor as an educational institution where the young are instructed in their religious heritage. The Israeli child is solely dependent upon the public school for anything he learns and understands about Judaism, apart from what he gets in his home environment and in his youth movement, and—in the case of the nonreligious—this often amounts to nothing.

Under the circumstances, one would have thought that the clericalist network of schools would only be too happy to attract as many nonreligious children as possible, if for no other reason than to "win their souls" for Orthodoxy. But nothing of the sort has, in fact, happened. True, the clericalists would like to get a larger allocation of funds for their educational network. They would like to see more buildings under their direction. But they do not care for children from nonreligious homes to be enrolled in their schools. If a child is not already fully observant, he does not belong! This, of course, bespeaks a certain fear on the part of the Orthodox, a sense of religious insecurity, which is also manifest in the fear which Orthodox parents have about their children's contact with nonreligious children outside of school hours.

The school system, therefore, far from providing the basis for a unified "Jewish culture," merely does its share for the perpetuation and ever increasing demarcation of "the two Israels." Nor can alleviation be found in those aspects of the religious tradition which the nonreligious have taken over and secularized. The national observance of Hanukkah, for example, with its candle-lighting, and its torch, lit in Modi'in, the birthplace of the Maccabees, and brought to Mount Zion, is a celebration in honor of the victorious Maccabees and of more recent attempts at Jewish "auto-emancipation," rather than, as in traditional Judaism, an occasion for gratitude to God. The same applies to the

Passover observance. The nonreligious collective settlements, in producing their own versions of the Passover *Haggadah*, are very careful indeed to eliminate all references to the deity. A "Blessing over the Bread," which praises "the farmer who brings bread forth from the earth," represents anything but a common ground with the religious sector of the population. On the contrary, it is offensive to any religious Jew, and not just to the Orthodox.

To round out the picture of the religious situation in Israel, we proceed to a brief description of the total religious spectrum as it is found in the Jewish State.

There have always been pious Orthodox Jews who came to Palestine in order to spend their last years on the soil of the Holy Land. To be buried in the Holy Land was considered a special virtue, and, according to a statement in the Talmud, it gave the person thus interred in holy soil an enviable degree of priority at the time of the eschatological Resurrection. Others came not only to die, but to spend their whole lives studying Torah and Talmud in the Holy Cities (i.e., Jerusalem, Hebron, Jaffa, Safed). They could always count on the support of Jews the world over, the latter considering the maintenance of perpetual Torah study in the Holy Land as one of the highest forms of philanthropy. Politically, the students of Torah and Talmud in the Holy Land had no aspirations whatsoever. On the contrary, they deemed all efforts directed at creating a Jewish State in Palestine to be a sinful interference with the messianic timetable of Almighty God. Economically, they made no attempt to be self-supporting.

Colonization was brought to the country by the pioneers coming from Polish and Russian backgrounds, beginning at the end of the last century, and continuing in waves through the first few decades of the present century. The East European Jewish youth who came as pioneers came with a background of rebellion against the traditional environment —traditional in economics, education, and religion. Although some of them may merely have been ritually nonobservant, thus being non-Orthodox rather than nonreligious, many, identifying religion with the forces of reaction, and combining their adherence to nationalism with an espousal of various forms of Marxist Socialism, adopted a downright antireligious stance. These nonreligious and antireligious pioneers, living in their communal settlements, were the backbone of Jewish Palestine's agricultural, economic, and cultural progress, under the British Mandate. They and their children dominate the State of Israel's labor unions, the ruling *Mapai* (Labor) Party, and the Marxist *Mapam* Party. Only the latter is dogmatically committed to an outspoken antireligious position. The *Mapai* Party and the General Federation of Labor Unions (*Histadruth*) have since made it clear that they are religiously neutral, having also made a number of concessions—in matters like observance of dietary laws and Sabbath restrictions—to Orthodox susceptibilities. However, in a country like Israel, where Jewish religion continues to be identified with religious Orthodoxy, the stance of neutrality in matters religious is still tantamount to a declaration of "nonreligiosity."

But not all the pioneers, and not all the communal settlements, were in rebellion against the inherited Orthodoxy. Though official Orthodoxy in Europe opposed the rising Zionist movement no less than did official Reform Judaism, there have been a number of Orthodox rabbis, even before the appearance of Theodor Herzl, who welcomed Jewish colonization efforts in Palestine, and who even preached the doctrine of a Jewish national revival in the ancient Homeland. Their rationale was that Jews need not wait passively for Messiah's coming, but could actually take the first concrete steps in clearing the redeemer's path. After the birth of Herzlian Zionism, this Orthodox-Zionist position crystallized in the ideology of the *Mizrachi* movement, a movement which, though a part of the World Zionist Organization, pursued its own additional aim of making Herzl's

Jewish State a state governed by the dictates of the Torah. A Socialist wing of this *Mizrachi* movement established its own collective settlements, in addition to furthering the building of *yeshivoth.*

The immigrants coming from Central Europe, from the nineteen-thirties on, fell into the already established religious categories of the country, without making any major efforts to perpetuate the liberal religious tradition in which many of them had grown up. The Oriental Jews, arriving since the fifties, naturally tend towards the established Orthodoxy, though, as we have already seen in connection with the educational problem, the *Mapai* (Labor) Party is making a fair bid to recruit members from among the Orientals as well. The avowed "neutrality" in religious matters may be a direct outcome of this recruiting drive.

Only fairly recently have attempts been made, and those primarily on the part of Jews of German and "Anglo-Saxon" provenance, to establish Reform and Conservative congregations more closely akin in their ideological (though, not necessarily, their ritual) patterns to central European and American prototypes. Though these attempts have aroused the ire of the Orthodox, and the amazement of incomprehension on the part of the nonreligious (who, like the Orthodox, have for too long been trained to think only in terms of "black or white"), the non-Orthodox religious groups are a relatively new phenomenon, and have not yet succeeded in attracting a sizeable proportion of the total population. Moreover, largely following a philosophy of liberalism in politics no less than in religion, these religious "dissidents" have refused to make their religion a matter of political maneuvering and machination.

Herein they differ from the other religious (and nonreligious) groups we have described. The latter fall into the following pattern: At the extreme right are the survivors, the descendants, and the (largely Hungarian and Polish) replenishments of those Jews who came to die and/or to study Torah in the Holy Land. They refuse to recognize the State of Israel altogether, and reject cooperation with Jews whose degree of ritual observance is less than their own. They likewise refuse to use the Hebrew language for secular purposes; and they consider themselves to be the true "Guardians of the City"—which is what the name *Natoré Kartha* means. For them, the concept of a Jewish State, which is not established by a divinely appointed Messiah, is sheer blasphemy—quite apart from the subjugation to a government largely composed of ritually non-observant Jews. As far as the *Natoré Kartha* are concerned, if only the Hashemite Kingdom of Jordan would let them, they would much prefer to live in a Jerusalem under non-Jewish administration than in a (heretical) "Jewish" Jerusalem. Though the "Guardians of the City" would be the last to acknowledge it, the government of the State of Israel treats them with an indulgent tolerance. It exempts their sons and daughters from compulsory military service. It refrains from interfering in the education of their young, and it turns a blind eye to their outbursts of intolerance which greet men and (particularly) women unsuitably attired in terms of their medieval standards of "modesty." Only with great reluctance does it, on occasion, send the police to deal with the riots provoked by Sabbath traffic passing through their streets. Since the "Guardians of the City" recognize neither the State of Israel nor its elected government, they do not participate in elections. Instead, they have a kind of "shadow government" of their own.

To the left of them are those Orthodox Jews who, without falling too far below "Guardians of the City" standards of ritual observance, have made their peace with the reality of the State of Israel. As members of the *Agudath Israel* Party, or of its workers' wing, the *Po'alé Agudath Israel*, they take part in the political life of the country, and even occupy seats in the Cabinet. Of course, their chief interest in Israeli politics is to win more and more concessions for Orthodoxy, and to write more and more religious law into the secular legislation of the country. There was a time when the *Agudath Israel* (originally a world-wide organization of Orthodox Jews) was fiercely opposed to Zionism, for reasons not dissimilar from those which prompt the *Natoré Kartha's* nonrecognition of the State of Israel. But, after the State was established, this party felt that its over-all aims and objectives could better be furthered within, rather than without, the established framework of the political machinery.

If we describe the next group, the offspring of the *Mizrachi* and its workers' wing, now together forming the National Religious Party, as being to the left of the *Agudath Israel*, then this description is based on historical backgrounds rather than on present-day realities. When the *Mizrachi* first came into existence, it became the butt par excellence of Orthodox attacks. Such attacks were almost a programmatic ingredient of *Agudath Israel* ideology. With all of their adherence to medieval Jewish legislation, the *Mizrachi* people were under the constant suspicion of pursuing reformist aims also in the field of religion. Indeed, the *Mizrachi* was more benign in its dealings with nonobservant Jews. It was also more favorably disposed toward secular education and general culture than the bulk (though not the German section) of the *Agudath Israel*. Moreover, in its collective settlements, it tried to come to terms with the conflicting demands of traditional law and modern exigencies. And it was a *Mizrachi* man, the late Rabbi J. L. Maimon, who advocated the convocation of a *sanhedrin*, a supreme religious council which, like its predecessor in the early Rabbinic period, would have the task of bringing religious law up to date. The fact that Rabbi Maimon's plea remained unheeded is indicative of the "turn to the right" which the *Mizrachi* movement has taken within recent years, a turn which makes its position practically identical with that of the *Agudath Israel*, and which enables the National Religious Party to join forces with the *Agudath Israel* in forming the "Religious Bloc" in Israel's politics and parliament.

To the left, again, is the *Mapai* (Labor) Party, which, as we have already seen, is religiously "neutral." But since, politically, it is not neutral, and since religion in Israel is a matter of politics, it is not an uncommon spectacle to see nonreligious and antireligious *Mapai* members of parliament voting for concessions to the Orthodox—in exchange, of course, for Orthodox votes in favor of *Mapai's* foreign and domestic policies.

To the left of *Mapai* there are the Marxist *Achduth Avodah* ("Unity of Labor"), *Mapam,* and Communist parties, with their traditional antireligious position.

We have left out of our account the (politically) right-wing *Heruth* Party, which has no religious program of its own, but which, like all right-wing parties the world over, tends, on occasion, to sympathize with clericalist aspirations. And we have not mentioned the Liberal Party, which is also religiously "neutral," because, on the one hand, it has members holding various religious views, and because, on the other hand, it is not numerically so significant. Yet it is within the Liberal Party that some of the more eloquent advocates of a "Separation of Church and State" (along Western democratic lines) are to be found. But we are speaking of individuals as individuals. The party itself, after three months of deliberations, has gone on record, in the summer of 1964, as being opposed to the seperation of state and religion, and as supporting the marriage and divorce laws at present in force in the State of Israel. (*The Jewish Chronicle,* London, July 24, 1964, p. 16.)

Nobody who has not witnessed the acrimony and the hatreds caused by political differences of opinion in the State of Israel could possibly imagine their character. Perhaps we can best visualize the situation by remembering that, some years ago, families found it impossible to live together because of the different political outlooks of their members and fences went up in collective settlements, separating the living quarters of those who voted for *Mapai* from the living quarters of those who voted for *Mapam.* If we, then, further bear in mind that religion in Israel is a matter of politics, we shall have to come to the regretful conclusion that religion is one of the least likely factors to provide cultural cohesion and a sense of common purpose and destiny for the citizens of the State of Israel. If anything, it represents one of the most divisive elements on the national scene.

One can view all this with a certain amount of sympathy, with a benign understanding of the growing pains of a young nation. All countries have had their initial problems; and Israel is a young country. It may yet solve its ethnic problems, its cultural problems, its educational problems, and even its religious problems. But, if it does, it will solve those problems against the background of present-day Israeli realities—just as there are problems which will find their solution in many of the other young countries which owe their political independence to recent United Nations decisions. What remains questionable is the assumption that Israel will find "Jewish" answers to those problems, rather than merely "Israeli" answers. What remains debatable is the proposition that past "Jewish" history leads up to a unilateral denouement, and that the venue of that denouement is the State of Israel, and the State of Israel alone.

No doubt, the State of Israel is one possibility which some heirs of the old Jewish way of life may choose for their self-fulfilment. But it is only one possibility, not the sole one. Its relationship to the past Jewish heritage is no more direct, and no more complete, and even no more authentic, than that of those Jews who, living as citizens of other sovereign states, elect to relegate the "national" aspects of Jewish existence to the historical past, preferring, instead, to single out the religious side of Jewish experience as the only meaningful criterion of their Jewish self-identification. Both the Israeli citizen and the American of the Jewish

faith are modern types, made possible by the fall of the
Ghetto walls. Neither is completely identical with the
Jewish type of the pre-Emancipation era. And both are
unable to put back the clock of historical development.

If these facts were honestly faced, there could be mutual
good will, respect, and understanding. But Zionist ideology
does not permit these facts to be faced; and the *raison d'état*
of the State of Israel lends no encouragement to viewing
the realities from the perspective we have adopted here.
Zionism still regards all Jews as potential citizens of the
State of Israel. And if, for tactical reasons, it has, of late,
somewhat toned down its political appeal to the Jews of
the West, it continues to enlist their support by means of
the twin claims of philanthropy and of the "Spiritual
Center."

CHAPTER TWO

Philanthropy — and Politics

The sources of Zionism are manifold. Among them is philanthropy. There have always been poor Jews in Palestine, and there have always been Jews outside Palestine who came to the support of individuals and of institutions in the Holy Land. The New Testament reports that even the Apostle Paul saw fit to solicit financial contributions from the churches established by him in Asia Minor for "the poor of Jerusalem." The charity collectors from the Holy Land were a frequent sight in all Jewish communities for a number of centuries; and the bearded and gaberdined "emissaries" from Jerusalem's Talmud academies can still be seen at frequent intervals even in the most unlikely American towns. Indeed, the first ordained rabbi to set foot on American soil, Hayyim Isaac Carrigal (1733-1777), was such an "emissary," and he became a friend of Ezra Stiles! Spanish and Portuguese Jewish congregations have a special synagogue official in charge of funds collected for "Terra Santa," and German and Polish Jews have long been familiar with charity boxes in their own homes, devoted to this or that institution in the Holy Land. The pious associations with the very names of Palestinian towns, fostered by the constant study of sacred literature, gave Palestinian institutions an honored place in the heart and in the pocketbook of the Jew. There can be no doubt that this ancient tradition has had its share in the success of modern Zionism.

But Zionism has had other sources as well. Until the Reformers of the nineteenth century began to understand Biblical prophecies in a figurative sense, the hope for a physical restoration of the Jewish People to the land of their fathers had always and universally been an integral part of the Synagogue's messianic doctrine. The king of the House of David, governing the whole world in truth and in righteousness, with the seat of his government in Zion, was not only a symbol for a world at peace, but an actual, concrete expectation. And the more Jewry suffered from persecution, the greater became their longing for a speedy Return to Zion. This longing inspired the poetry of the great Spanish-Jewish poet-philosopher, Judah Halevi (ca. 1086-1145), who bewailed the fact that he had to live "in the farthest West," while his "heart was in the East." But it also inspired the deceptions and the intrigues of the many pseudo-messiahs who never failed to gain followers among those who were "looking to salvation."

While, as we have seen in Chapter One, the first reaction of traditional Judaism to modern Zionism was negative, since it regarded Zionism as a sinful interference on the part of man with the long-range plans of God, we may be reasonably sure that, in many circles, Zionism was able to "cash in" on the Jewish messianic hope. There are secular Zionists who already see in the establishment of the State of Israel *the* fulfilment of the millennial Jewish messianic hope. There are religious Zionists who are a little more circumspect, and who are satisfied in seeing the modern State of Israel as only "the Beginning of the Redemption." But the fact remains that, when the State was established, in 1948, a member of the Rabbinical Court of London, England, sounded the *shofar*—traditionally regarded as a signal of Messiah's arrival.

Another source of Zionism, one to which we shall devote Chapter Three, was the striving for a "Spiritual Center." Secularized Jews in Eastern Europe, and, in particular, one

Asher Ginzburg, who wrote under the pseudonym of "Achad Ha'Am," saw the dissolution of traditional religious ties, and despaired of the possibility of creating a secularized Jewish culture either in Eastern Europe (where the Jews were too poor and too persecuted) or in the West (where the Jews were already far too "assimilated" to non-Jewish culture). There remained only one hope: to establish a spiritual, or cultural, center for world Jewry on Palestinian soil, where the Hebrew language could be revived, and where a Hebrew culture could come into being. This aspiration did not necessarily envisage any large-scale immigration of Jews to Palestine, or the dissolution of the Jewish communities in the Diaspora. On the contrary, it was to be precisely the function of the Palestinian Spiritual Center to help in the revival of Jewish culture elsewhere. The imagery employed was one of a circle, with its center and its periphery. It was "Achad Ha'Am" who voiced the opinion that one Palestinian institution of higher learning was of greater importance than a hundred agricultural settlements.

Yet there were others to whom the agricultural settlements were of primary importance. And this for many reasons. For one thing, there was a striving for a "return to the soil," for greater contact with Nature, of a kind made impossible by the restrictive Russian legislation governing Jewish settlement. For another, a life in agriculture promised a "normalization" of the economic and professional structure of Jewish living. For a third, it represented an opportunity to put into practice one's Socialist ideology. All of this, again, was not necessarily connected with—in fact, much of it antedated—the formulation of an over-all program aiming at the creation of an independent Jewish State.

But such a program was, in due course, formulated; and that by men like Leon Pinsker (1821-1891), Theodor Herzl (1860-1904), and Max Nordau (1849-1923). Once it was formulated, it overshadowed all the contributing factors which went into the making of Zionism, though some of them, in part, were incorporated. Political Zionism, or "State Zionism," arose as a reaction to anti-Semitism. It granted the anti-Semitic assumption that the Jews were a "foreign body" among their "host-peoples." It saw no other solution to the problem of anti-Semitism than the total removal of the Jews from the lands of the non-Jews to a country of their own. For, according to this analysis, wherever else Jews settle in appreciable numbers, they bring the seeds of anti-Semitism with them. For the Jews are indeed a nation, a nation like the British nation, or the French nation, or the German nation. But they are a nation which, for some two thousand years, has been leading a most unnatural kind of existence—a "nation in exile," a nation without its Homeland. All problems would be solved once this Jewish nation would take its place among the family of nations, based upon its own sovereign state.

Interestingly enough, though Palestine figured in the search for a suitable territory, it was not the only place which was mentioned in this connection. Pinsker thought of either Palestine or of the Argentine. Herzl, for a time, was willing to settle for Uganda. At this point, the other sources of Zionism came into play, the pious memories, and the historical associations, championed particularly by the Russian Zionists. From the beginning of the present century there was no longer any doubt that the Homeland of the Jewish nation could only be Palestine. ("Achad Ha'Am" was virtually the only Zionist leader in those early days who paid any attention to the fact that Palestine was not an uninhabited territory, that there was indeed an Arab population, and that the existence of this Arab population must be taken into consideration in any long-range plans for Jewish settlement in Palestine. His warning was widely ignored, though men like Martin Buber and Judah L. Magnes were to reiterate it in our own day.)

The early days of political Zionism were days of great internal struggles. What was to be given priority in the

scale of values of the organization? Was it to be the continuation of the work of quiet colonization, which had already
begun before the World Zionist Organization had come into
existence, or was it to be the political negotiations with
the world powers, leading to an official acquisition of Palestine by the Jewish nation? Was it to be political activity, or
was it to be—as Martin Buber insisted—cultural work? Was
the State to be a secular state, as Herzl anticipated, or was
it to be governed by Torah law, as the *Mizrachi* faction advocated? And, once the Balfour Declaration, in 1917, promised
the British government's support for a Jewish National Home
"in Palestine," was one to be satisfied to work within those
limits, or was the aim of Zionism to be a sovereign Jewish
State on both banks of the river Jordan, if necessary, to be
conquered by force of arms, as advocated by the Zionist-
Revisionists?

While all of this was being discussed, the German government, in 1933, adopted anti-Semitism as an official policy
of the German *Reich*—with consequences which will not be
forgotten as long as Jewish history is being written. More
slowly than one would have wished from the vantage point
of hindsight it dawned on the German Jews that they would
have to emigrate from their fatherland. Palestine loomed on
the horizon as a possible and likely haven of refuge. The
gates of too many other countries were closed to Jewish
refugees. Under the circumstances, many ideological battles
of the past were forgotten, and Jews of all shades of opinion
cooperated in supporting the Jewish colonization effort in
Palestine.

Yet Palestine was then under the British Mandate, and
the British were committed to keeping the peace of that
country—in addition to being encumbered by a number of
promises they had also made to the Arab inhabitants of
Palestine. This led to a limitation of the number of Jews
who could annually be admitted into the country. In turn,
this led to renewed Zionist insistence upon an independent

and sovereign Jewish State, with unlimited Jewish immigration.

Perhaps it can be said—again from the vantage point of hindsight—that, throughout those critical years, the Zionist endeavor was directed, not so much toward the saving of Jewish lives—which could have been accomplished by pressing for a liberalization of immigration policies in the free countries—as toward the political aim of establishing a Jewish State in Palestine. Zionists have always understood how to harness the philanthropic impulses of non-Zionists to the Zionist cause. The late Chaim Weizmann, great Zionist leader and first president of the State of Israel, did not even hesitate to admit that, in the early days of Zionism, "those wealthy Jews who could not wholly divorce themselves from a feeling of responsibility toward their people" were induced to make "philanthropic" contributions which, without their knowledge, would serve the nationalist cause. "To them the university-to-be in Jerusalem was philanthropy, which did not compromise them; to us it was nationalist renaissance. They would give—with disclaimers; we would accept—with reservations." (Chaim Weizmann, *Trial and Error*. New York, Harper and Brothers, 1949, p. 75.) Now, however, it was not merely a question of cultural institutions. Zionism was presented as *the* means of saving Jewish lives; and opposition to Zionism by Jews was largely silenced. After all, opposing Jewish colonization endeavors at a time like that would have been tantamount to condemning Jews to certain death. Thus the cooperation of Jews was obtained who shared neither the Zionists' basic assumptions nor the Zionists' political aims.

This situation did not change even after the end of World War II. Now it became a question, a burning question, of finding a haven of refuge for the pitiful remnants of the Nazi holocaust, eagerly awaiting their liberation from the Displaced Persons camps of Europe. Whether all of them initially insisted upon a Palestinian destination, or whether they were induced to make this choice by a wide network of Zionist agents then active throughout Europe, is a question we need not consider now. The fact remains that, to the world at large, it was made clear that the inhabitants of the Displaced Persons camps *had* to be taken to Palestine.

But Palestine was still under British administration, and Britain was still committed to the Arabs as much as to the Jews, and Britain still refused to permit any sudden mass immigration of Jews into Palestine. This led to the organization of an illegal immigration. It led to the formation of Jewish terrorist groups in Palestine, trying to make the place "too hot" for the British. And it led to the concentrated efforts to get the Zionist aim of an independent Jewish State, internationally recognized, once and for all established.

The climate was favorable. The world, after Auschwitz and Buchenwald, had a guilty conscience about the Jews. The sight of refugee ships, arriving at the Palestinian coast, being turned back by the British Navy, and of illegal immigrants being interned in Cyprus, was too much to stomach. By 1947, the United Nations was amenable to the creation of a Jewish State, and Britain had had enough. The partition of Palestine into Jewish and Arab sections was approved, and the State of Israel came into existence in May 1948. It was immediately attacked by the Arabs, but, through various feats of heroism, it managed to maintain itself, and to win its War of Independence. The Jewish State was now prepared to welcome with open arms any Jew who seeks admission. Many sought it. Many more had to seek it. And the fact that, after 1948, so many *had* to seek it leads us to a renewed investigation of the ratio of philanthropy to nationalist politics in the drive which led to the establishment of the State of Israel.

That the Arabs would not take kindly to the establishment of a Jewish State in Palestine could have been predicted. There was no lack of Arab warnings; and, in a long history of rioting, the Arabs had already demonstrated how they would react to the achievement of the Zionist aim. That Israel was able to beat the Arabs on the field of battle was, however, only one side of the picture. There were also large and long-established Jewish settlements in the various Muslim countries, and the Zionist politicians, astute as they are in so many realms, must have known that the Arabs would take reprisals, that the Jews in Muslim lands would immediately be cast in the role of hostages. But, whether the Zionist politicians were aware of this or not (and, perhaps, they welcomed, rather than feared, a forced mass immigration of Jews from Muslim countries), a reckoning with the fate of the Jewish population of Muslim countries is an inescapable part of dealing with the creation of the Jewish State from a philanthropic, rather than from a political, point of view. And it is on the basis of philanthropy that the major Zionist appeal is currently being made to the Jews of the United States.

To deal with this aspect of the situation, we are using figures published by the government of Israel itself, in the *Statistical Abstract of Israel* No. 14 (1963), page 110. From these statistics it appears that, between May 15, 1948 and December 31, 1948, 76,554 immigrants went from Europe to Israel. For 1949, the figure of European immigrants is 121,753. For 1951, it is 49,533. We must assume that these figures represent those survivors of the concentration camps who were anxiously waiting to get out of their Displaced Persons camps in Europe. It will be remembered that it was largely on their behalf that the efforts to establish an independent Jewish State in Palestine were brought to a head.

But, in 1949, when 121,753 immigrants came from Europe, 110,780 immigrants came from Muslim countries (39,156 from Africa; 71,624 from Asia). In 1951, when 49,533 immigrants came from Europe, 123,449 came from Muslim countries (20,123 from Africa; 103,326 from Asia). In 1955, when the immigration from Europe had dwindled down to 1,942, the immigration from Muslim countries still stood at

33,736 (32,413 from Africa; 1,323 from Asia). Obviously, the very existence of the State of Israel had placed Jewish survival in the Muslim world in jeopardy. This is the real price paid for the establishment of the Jewish State.

The total figures are even more instructive. For the period from May 15, 1948 through December 31, 1961, we hear of 466,812 immigrants coming from Europe, America, and Oceania (the number of immigrants from the latter two regions is relatively insignificant). But we also hear of 529,078 immigrants coming to Israel during the same period from Asia and Africa. The European figures amount to 46.9 per cent of the total, whereas the Asian and African figures come to 53.1 per cent!

Allowing for the possibility that there might have been some immigration to Israel from Asian and African countries even without the special anti-Jewish measures taken by the Arab governments, just as some of the immigrants from Europe do not fall into the category of survivors of the concentration camps, we are still left with some rather disturbing results. If philanthropy be our criterion, then the conclusion has to be that Jewish existence in the Muslim world was sacrificed in order to get the Jewish Displaced Persons out of Europe! To this must be added the consideration that, although some of the latter have since returned to Europe, or moved on to the American continent, no such return is possible for the Jews from Arab countries.

If philanthropy be our criterion, then how do we calculate the speedy relief afforded the people in the Displaced Persons camps as against the uprooting of half a million Asian and African Jews, plus the virtual dissolution of Jewish life in the Muslim world? The figures speak for themselves. They simply rule out philanthropy as the true motivation for the whole enterprise.

But if politics, rather than philanthropy, were the real motivation, then the whole picture would fall into focus. Not only is the dissolution of Jewish settlements in the Diaspora something which need not be regretted; it is actually a part of Zionism's "fulfilment." In *The Jerusalem Post* of July 21, 1964 (page 3, columns 7 and 8), Nissim Rejwan, who was personally involved in the Iraqi immigration to Israel, has some very enlightening things to say on that subject. He states that the establishment of the State of Israel led to the arrest of known Zionists in Iraq, and soon to a penalizing of the whole Iraqi Jewish community. Nevertheless, according to Rejwan, the Jewish emigration from Iraq, far from being the "rescue immigration" to Israel of the conventional reports, was, in actual fact, a result of "intensive Zionist activity inside Iraq." "It was the pressure of the Jews themselves . . . that finally forced the hand of the authorities."

From the Zionist point of view, therefore, the thousands of refugees from the Muslim world are not so many additional charity cases with which Israeli and world Jewry are being burdened, but they furnish the much-needed manpower for the Israeli State and its armed forces. Things have merely been going according to plan! As if to substantiate our analysis, Mr. S. Z. Shragai, head of the Aliyah Department of the Jewish Agency, "expressed regret" when Jewish circles in the United States succeeded in getting the U.S. State Department to open the doors of America to one thousand Jewish children from Algeria. Mr. Shragai "appealed to all those concerned with the transfer of Orthodox children to the United States to redirect them to Israel." (*The Jewish Chronicle*, London, August 10, 1962, page 24.) And when, during the summer of 1962, it had become apparent that many Algerian Jews were preferring to move to France instead of to Israel, speaker after speaker at the Third Hebrew World Congress, held in Jerusalem at that time, referred to the "tragedy" of the Algerian Jews' choice.

Yet it must be frankly admitted that, during the greater part of its history, Zionism never concealed its true political motivations. "Conquer the communities!" was the motto from the very beginning of organized political Zionism. (Cf. Alex Bein, *Theodore Herzl—A Biography*. Philadelphia, Jewish Publication Society, 1941, pp. 271f.) And the "conquest" of the communities implied the Zionist leadership of Jewish congregations and institutions. It meant gaining control of the channels of Jewish education. It meant, finally, recruiting and training Jewish youth for emigration to Palestine.

One of the primary communities to be "conquered" was and is, of course, the Jewish community of the United States of America; and, to a very large extent, the "conquest" has succeeded. But American Jews balked at one thing: personal commitment to emigration to the Jewish State. American Jews, in no small number, also found it impossible to agree to something else: the Zionist dogma (as distinct from the religious dogma about which more will be said in our fourth chapter) which maintains that American Jews are living "in exile," and that the American Jewish community, like all other Diaspora communities, is doomed to extinction.

The average American Zionist, whose Zionism is indeed primarily a matter of philanthropy, of supporting Jewish refugees in the one country willing to admit them in large numbers, was deeply hurt each time Israel's former Prime Minister, Mr. David Ben-Gurion, made a speech calling for the immigration of American Jews, and denying the right of calling themselves "Zionists" to all who did not plan to settle in the Jewish State. Yet Mr. Ben-Gurion was only reiterating classical Zionist doctrine!

The money contributed by American Jews is so essential to the welfare and to the very survival of Zionism that the tone in which American Jews are being addressed has now been considerably softened. Direct appeals calling for mass emigration from America have become rare—though the networks of Hebrew day schools and various Zionist youth movements have not relinquished their endeavor to make American Jewish children believe that the only place where

Jews are "really" at home is in the State of Israel. By and large, the Zionist leadership is content to let Zionism in America be identified with philanthropy. Philanthropy is the "pitch" of the speeches made at United Jewish Appeal functions. Philanthropy is the theme of the films shown at them. And philanthropy is the rallying point of American Jewish women who contribute their time, their energy, and their (and their husbands') funds to the Hadassah organization.

Who could possibly object to sending medical equipment to an underdeveloped country? (That would be like being against motherhood!) Who could raise his voice against the training of physicians and the extension of medical services? And who, on a tourist trip to Israel, could resist the sight of the magnificent Hadassah Hospital outside of Jerusalem—with its famous Chagall windows as an added attraction? No, there is no doubt that the Hadassah organization is doing splendid philanthropic and humanitarian work.

Few members of Hadassah will have taken the trouble to read the small print on their membership cards. There, the organization is described as "The Women's Zionist Organization of America, Inc." Innocent words, those—until we begin to realize that the Zionist Organization of America is a *political* organization, and that the number of membership cards issued becomes a matter of "counting noses" for political-pressure tactics. And, for that matter, neither the Zionist Organization of America, nor its Hadassah branch, have so far, *in principle*, rejected the long-range Zionist aim of mass emigration from America to Israel. Hadassah has merely been on record as favoring the soft-pedaling of this aspect of Zionist "self-fulfilment" for the time being, the present moment not being considered too propitious for emphasizing this particular theme.

Few members of Hadassah will know this. The American Jew's philanthropic concern blinds him to the political implications. Membership in Hadassah, at that, has perhaps still the fewest political implications. There are actually counterparts to Israel's political parties on the American Jewish scene. The Labor Zionist Organization of America identifies itself with Israel's *Mapai* Party, just as the American Jewish youth organization, *Hashomer Hatza'ir*, represents the ideology of the Israeli *Mapam* Party, and the American *Mizrachi* organization is linked to the Religious Bloc in Israel. Again, it is not to be assumed that many, or perhaps even most, of the American Jews who join such organizations have anything more in mind than giving their philanthropic support to agricultural settlers in Israel, or to the religious endeavors of the Israeli pioneers. But the organizations in question are political parties, and those who are willing to read the "small print" could easily convince themselves of this.

It is, however, not in the interest of Zionist leadership, either in Israel or in the United States, to ruin the philanthropic illusion of American Jews. (Mr. Ben-Gurion is the exception that proves the rule.) Philanthropy is one of the chief expressions of "Jewishness" for American Jews. The place of honor occupied in the Jewish life of other times and other climes by the Torah scholar is assigned, in American Jewry, to the big donor and contributor. The pressure tactics employed by the fund-raising organizations—such as the public announcements at gala dinners of the amounts contributed—have had a profound effect on American Jewry's mores and scale of values, a state of affairs greatly aided by the way of life of an "other-directed" society. American Jews *need* the whole apparatus of the welfare funds, the United Jewish Appeal, Israel Bonds, etc., in order to establish their position in the community. One might even say that, if the needs of Israel (which, incidentally, are very real) did not already exist, something like them would have to be invented! Under the circumstances, Zion-

ism, in philanthropic garb, has done very well indeed by
American Jews; and a situation bereft of such activities
simply could not be imagined.

The needs of Israeli Jews, as we have indicated, are very
real indeed. The tourist who "sees" the country in a week
or two may only see the highspots. The visitor who stays
longer will not fail to be moved by the abject poverty of
large sections of the population. Housing, clothing and
better educational and medical facilities are needed. Institutions are needed to take the young people off the streets,
particularly at night and on weekends. All these are causes
to which American Jewish charity might well be directed.
The question is only whether American Jewish philanthropy
is best directed through political channels. And, as long as
the collection and the transfer and the distribution of funds
are left to political organizations, both in the United States
and in Israel, the charitable contributions of American Jews
are made to serve political ends as well.

There is, of course, an argument which would present
Zionism itself as a philanthropic endeavor. After all, the
founders of political Zionism were obsessed by, what they
called, the *Juden-Not*—the very real and physical needs of
Jews, caused by political and economic anti-Semitism.
Zionism, in fact, came into being as an antidote, to bring
relief to Jewish suffering. Thus, it is not the existence of
needy Jews in Israel which is worthy of philanthropic support, but the political machinery of Zionism and the State
of Israel itself, seeing that this machinery has the function
of "solving" the "Jewish Problem."

The achievements of Zionism in this area have been im-
pressive. The State of Israel has indeed provided a very
necessary haven of refuge for persecuted Jews, and it has
furnished the wherewithal enabling those refugees to begin
a new life. But we must not forget that many of the refugees,
as has been established on the basis of statistics earlier in
this chapter, are themselves the innocent victims of Arab re-

actions to Zionist achievements. The victory of Zionism is also responsible for the inability of Jews to travel freely in the Near and Middle East. It is responsible, too, for the pitiful state of the remaining Jews in Muslim countries.

The founders of political Zionism had a glorious dream. They were sure that the existence of an independent Jewish State would afford protection to Jews the world over—that is, even to those Jews who, for some reason or other, elected to remain in the Diaspora. If such a Jew were hurt or insulted, the ambassador of the Jewish State would make immediate representations to the government concerned, and justice would be done. But this dream did not reckon with the realities of modern power politics. Far from protecting the rights of the Jews in the Diaspora, the Jewish State is constantly enlisting the good offices of the Diaspora Jews for the purpose of insuring its own existence.

But the old philosophy lives on. The old notion that the "Jewish Problem" can only be "solved" in an independent Jewish State is still responsible for the lack of concentrated effort to work for, and to think of the resettlement of Jewish refugees in terms other than those of the State of Israel. If a thousand Jewish children from Algeria find refuge in the United States of America, then "regret" is expressed by a high official of an organization which obtains its funds through philanthropic contributions!

Yes, there is an element of philanthropy in Zionism. But read the "small print," and you will find that it is philanthropy—and politics. There is a stretch of the road along which the interests of Zionism and the interests of philanthropy coalesce. But there comes a point where this road branches out into two separate roads, one marked "Philanthropy," the other, "Politics." Modern Jewish history has now reached the bifurcation of the road. It will not do to strut along toward a political destination, if one's aim is that of philanthropy. Only the blind and the careless do so.

American Jews, like most other Americans, are basically

pragmatists. They are impressed by facts. They like to see concrete results. They are not much given to reading the "small print," and ideological considerations are of very little interest to them. But, unless they soon take time out to study the "small print," unless they take the trouble to familiarize themselves with Zionist ideology, they may find themselves unwittingly pursuing aims and objectives which are completely foreign to their own basic outlook and to their own best interest.

In the second century before the Common Era, the Seleucid king Antiochus Epiphanes threw his authority and his armed forces behind the attempt to force the Jewish community of Palestine into Hellenistic patterns of life and religion. Many of those who remained attached to their ancestral faith fled into the hills, there to practice, under privations but with comparative freedom, the dictates of their inherited religion. This group was known as the *Hasidim*, or "the Pietists." When Judah the Maccabee gathered his forces to fight compulsory Hellenization on the field of battle, the "Pietists" came out into the open, and enlisted in the Maccabee's ranks. But the Hasmoneans (which was the family name of Judah the Maccabee) did more than liberate and purify the Jerusalem Temple. They did more than wrest from their Syrian overlords the right to worship according to the ancestral pattern. They also established an independent Jewish kingdom. They also founded a dynasty of Hasmonean priest-kings. And they also engaged in wars of conquest. Yet, when these dynastic and territorial ambitions of the Hasmoneans became evident, the "Pietists" took their leave. They had joined the ranks of the Maccabee solely for the purpose of establishing the freedom of the Jewish religion in Palestine. They would have no traffic with any dynastic ambitions or territorial conquests. They pursued their nonpolitical religious interests. But it was through their teachings that the foundations of later Rabbinic Judaism were laid, a Judaism which survived the destruction of

Temple and State, two centuries later, and which is the basis of all modern forms of Judaism as well.

Vis-à-vis the aspiration of Zionism, the role of American Jewry could very well be analogous to the role of the "Pietists" in relation to the Hasmoneans. Just as there could be wholehearted cooperation with Zionism as long as Zionism appeared to be the best way of helping suffering Jews, so there could now be a frank taking of leave, once it is realized that the political aims and objectives of Zionism and the Zionist State do not necessarily coincide with the philanthropic objectives of American Jewry.

Let the Zionist organizations and political parties (or what will remain of them) confine themselves to the promotion of their political aims, and to the collection of such funds as may be essential to their furtherance. But let the aims of philanthropy henceforth be pursued through agencies which have no connection whatsoever with political platforms and philosophies. If it be a question of finding a haven of refuge for uprooted people, then let those agencies investigate what can be done in the State of Israel. But let them also not close their eyes to other possibilities. And let the direction of such agencies remain entirely in the hands of Americans. The views of the government of the State of Israel and of the Zionist Organization may, on occasion, be solicited; but under no circumstances will those agencies be guided by purely political considerations. And let independent studies be made in Israel, by economists, sociologists, educationists, medical experts, and social scientists, of how the American Jewish charity dollar could best be invested in the State of Israel. What are the needs in education and in vocational training? What can be done to get the young people off the streets? How can medical services be improved? How can the housing shortage be alleviated? These and similar questions must and can be studied and answered without reference to doctrinal considerations. And one other question, one which, in the existing setup, could not even be brought up: what can be done by way of resettlement for those immigrants who, for one reason or another (economic, psychological, medical), cannot adjust to the Israeli environment?

It goes without saying that these American charitable agencies will have to maintain their own offices and distribution centers in Israel, staffed by American personnel free from any Israeli political attachments. If the prospect of setting up such a network of agencies appears to be formidable and too costly, one need only compare it with the present structure and organizational expenditure of the Zionist apparatus, with all of its factional duplication of efforts, as it came to light during the recent Congressional investigation of the Jewish Agency. With fewer entanglements and with wider scope than the present politically controlled organizations, the philanthropic agencies we suggest could, at one and the same time, unify the charitable endeavors of American Jewry by obliterating the current political and ideological barriers, and reestablish the old Jewish tradition which liked to link philanthropy with the Holy Land.

CHAPTER THREE

The Spiritual Center

The philanthropic appeal, in both its legitimate and in its dubious aspects, is not the only appeal which the State of Israel and the Zionist Organization address to the Jews of the Diaspora. Even in the absence of more direct ideological avowals of Jewish nationalism, the philanthropic appeal is often coupled with, or supplemented by, a presentation of the State of Israel as the "Spiritual Center" of world Jewry. This latter can, on occasion, take the form of a denial of the possibility of a "full Jewish life" in any place but the State of Israel. More often than not it is satisfied with leaving the impression that world Jewry is spiritually sustained by what is going on in the State of Israel.

It will be our task here to examine this impression and this claim, both in regard to its validity in terms of the Israeli scene and from the point of view of Diaspora Jewish existence. The phrase "Spiritual Center" sounds so high-minded and so noble that very few attempts have been made before now to examine its objective content.

To begin with, we shall need a more adequate description of what is meant by "spiritual." The term can have one of two meanings, or a combination of both. It could either refer to the cultural endeavor in general, or it could have reference to more narrowly "religious" concerns. It could also denote a combination of the two. As far as secular Jewish culture is concerned, we have already dealt with the problem in Chapter One. There we noted that, apart from religion, it is practically impossible to speak about a "Jewish culture," i.e., of a culture shared by Jews of all geographical and ethnic backgrounds. We also noted that a distinct *Israeli* culture was indeed in the process of becoming. But we also indicated the great difficulty experienced by the cultural apostles of the State of Israel in getting their local culture identified with "Jewish culture" per se. Yet it is upon the success of such an identification that the claim made for the State of Israel as *the* "Spiritual Center" is predicated.

If, for example, I agree that "Jewish culture" means the treatment of Israeli themes and the use of the Hebrew language, then I shall also be forced to agree that the pursuit of such a culture is infinitely easier in the State of Israel than it would be in the American Middle West or in the provincial centers of England. The only trouble is that the initial agreement is already a case of begging the question.

Again, if I identify "Jewish culture" with the folkways and the mores of the East European Jewish environment of yesteryear, I may also find the pursuit of such a culture greatly facilitated in the larger company of fellow East Europeans which I am liable to encounter within the borders of the State of Israel. (New York, though, may still be a lively competitor.) Yet, as we have seen in Chapter One, the vast aggregate of cultural and ethnic backgrounds, provided by the State of Israel itself, should put us on our guard when it comes to identifying any one cultural heritage with *the* "Jewish culture."

On the other hand, we do not deny the possibility that the distinctive *Israeli* culture which is now developing could appeal to people in the United States, and, among them, also to American Jews. There are Americans whose love for French, or Italian, or Mexican culture equals, if it does not exceed, their love for their own cultural heritage.

Such people may stock their libraries with French, Italian, or Spanish volumes. They may make a few, or frequent, trips to Paris, Rome, or Mexico City. But, as long as they do not move their residence permanently to France, Italy, or Mexico, that interest in foreign cultures will never be more than a hobby. Possibly an absorbing hobby, but a hobby just the same. On that level, an Israeli culture, and a "Spiritual Center" to go with it, could easily be contemplated. But that is not what the Zionists have in mind. An American may, or may not, be interested in French culture. Nobody, not even the cultural attaché of the French embassy, can tell him that he *must* be interested. Not so the Zionists. According to them, the American Jew *must* be interested in Israeli culture and in the Israeli "Spiritual Center," because such an interest follows logically from one's Jewish self-identification.

It is obvious, of course, that such an interest does not follow logically at all. It is an interest which must be acquired first; and a vast machinery of propaganda—including youth movements, Jewish day schools, religious school textbooks, summer camps, partially underwritten trips to Israel—is geared to the creation of this particular interest. Even the attempt in supposedly "religious" circles to emphasize the modern spoken Hebrew idiom at the expense of the study of classical religious texts is a manifestation of this propaganda endeavor to create an interest in Israeli culture.

This endeavor has not been without its successes. It has been successful in an inverse ratio to the spiritual poverty of organized Jewish religious life in the United States—a subject to which we shall have to return later in this book. And the successes have not been without their dire results upon Jewish existence in America. Zionist aims notwithstanding, the vast majority of those reached by the propaganda apparatus have not decided to emigrate to the State of Israel. Their interest, native or acquired, in Israeli culture has remained on the level of a hobby. Even the interest in the "revived Hebrew language" has not led to much more than an ability to converse about the weather in Hebrew. There is little reading of serious Hebrew literature in America; and the readership of Hebrew publications in the States has gone down in spite of the lively interest sponsored by Zionist propaganda. *HADOAR*, the Hebrew weekly published in New York, has found itself in increasing financial straits with the gradual demise of its old-time readers of East European provenance. Its readership has not increased in proportion to the wide mushrooming of "Hebrew-Speaking Circles" throughout the United States. In other words, the hobby is not even an absorbing one!

But, at the same time, with an Israel-oriented education in the Jewish day schools, many American Jewish children are brought up to believe that a "real Jewish life" is possible only in Israel. If they decide to remain in America, they will be satisfied with a vicarious kind of Judaism—one which consists of financial contributions to Israel, combined with a sense of inferiority and complete passivity in terms of Jewish creativity in America. This tendency has already been much in evidence.

To return to our starting point, let us repeat, then, the conclusion that the need for a secular "Spiritual Center" in Israel is predicated upon the assumption that the distinct Israeli culture now being created in the State of Israel is "Jewish culture," and, therefore, meaningful to Jews of all cultural and ethnic backgrounds. We have found no reason to accept such an assumption. Furthermore, one of the moot questions we touched on in Chapter One is the one about the possibility of a "Jewish culture" as such, one, that is to say, which is distinct from the religious expression of Judaism.

It is, then, quite natural that, when the Zionist appeal for a secular "Spiritual Center" is made to the Jew of the

Diaspora, the latter is often quite unable to dissociate such a concept from the religious overtones and undertones which a mention of the land of the Patriarchs and Prophets always stirs up in the hearts of the believers. The culture produced in Israel may result in such choice statements as that of the Hebrew writer Jonathan Ratosh, "Israel will be destroyed unless we come to realize that the Jewish religion and the Hebrew nation are not identical" (*Hadassah Magazine,* December, 1963, page 4), but the unsuspecting recipient of Zionist propaganda will continue to think of Zion and Jerusalem in terms of their Biblical and liturgical associations.

What, therefore, can be said about the "Spiritual Center" from the point of view of its religious potential? If Judaism were an hierarchical religion, a case could be made out in favor of a kind of Jewish Vatican with its seat in Zion. But Judaism, as it has developed, is *not* an hierarchical religion; at least the more modern forms of the faith, such as Conservatism and Reform, have rejected any such pretensions. It is, moreover, rather doubtful whether, after the cessation of the Jewish High Priesthood, if not before, Judaism ever presented a suitable parallel to the organization of the Roman Catholic Church. Perhaps the nearest Judaism has come to it (and even that still represents some distance) was in its Orthodox wing; and it is the Orthodox Jews who might have most to gain from the establishment of a supreme ecclesiastical authority situated in Jerusalem. The experiment has already been advocated; and among its advocates was no less a person than the first Minister for Religious Affairs of the State of Israel, the late Rabbi J. L. Maimon.

What Rabbi Maimon had in view was the reconstitution of the *sanhedrin,* the supreme legislative Jewish authority of the early Rabbinic period. Only a *sanhedrin,* he felt, could adjust the requirements of traditional Jewish law to the needs and exigencies of modern times; and it was just such an adjustment which, according to Rabbi Maimon, the modern State of Israel called for.

The plan to reconstitute the *sanhedrin* came to nought. It became a victim of the opposition within the ranks of Orthodoxy itself. To that opposition, any thought of "adjusting" Jewish law sounded heretical, and suggested the dread heresy of Reform. Technically, the opposition couched its argument in terms of Ordination requirements, or the absence thereof. The kind of Ordination, which, in ancient times, qualified a man to sit in the *sanhedrin,* had ceased many centuries ago. There was an attempt to revive it in Palestine, in the sixteenth century; but this attempt came to grief, too. One of the theologico-legalistic points at issue is whether Ordination can be reintroduced, and the *sanhedrin* reconstituted, prior to the advent of Messiah, or whether Messiah's coming is itself a prerequisite for a reconstituted *sanhedrin.* Both sides of the question could be argued on the basis of traditional Jewish sources, and both sides have found their advocates. Rabbi Maimon, in his proposal, represented the more progressive *Mizrachi* wing of Israel's "Religious Bloc." The defeat of Rabbi Maimon's proposal is indicative of the "turn to the right" of which we have already spoken in connection with the religious scene in Israel.

But even if Rabbi Maimon and his adherents could have cleared the first hurdle, the practical value of the *sanhedrin* plan would still not have been automatically assured. Contrary to appearances, Jewish Orthodoxy is anything but a monolithic structure. Even if they would have agreed to the reconvening of the *sanhedrin,* would the representatives of East European Orthodoxy have admitted to *sanhedrin* membership those Orthodox rabbis from a Western background who combine their Rabbinic learning with a secular Ph.D. degree? And, if they would not have agreed, how representative would that *sanhedrin* have been? Moreover, speaking of being representative, Rabbi Maimon and his followers, of course, never even contemplated non-Orthodox representatives in their planned *sanhedrin*! In terms of twentieth-century Jewish realities, Rabbi Maimon's *sanhedrin*, even if the proposal had been accepted, would have had little more than a parochial significance.

It has indeed been argued that the reconvening of the *sanhedrin* would have been no guarantee for the modernization of Jewish law. The members of that *sanhedrin* would have been as liable to give a strict, as a lenient, interpretation to Jewish law—this, and something else. Many of the basic and fundamental changes in Jewish law called for by modern life do not require the existence of a *sanhedrin* at all. They could be instituted by individual rabbis holding the modern form of Ordination. They could be strengthened by local Rabbinical Courts and Councils. No *sanhedrin* ever authorized the legal codes of Maimonides or Joseph Caro, or stood behind the many Rabbinic *responsa* by means of which Jewish law was kept flexible throughout the centuries. But the fact remains that, within more recent centuries, the Orthodox rabbinate has become more timid, less inclined to make the kind of innovation which, in terms of the law itself, they would have been entitled to make even without benefit of *sanhedrin*. This timidity might merely have been perpetuated by the modern *sanhedrin*. Or it might not. The fact that the *sanhedrin* was never reconvened in the first place would, however, incline us to suspect a preponderance of timidity.

With the *sanhedrin* of such doubtful value even to the Orthodox themselves, it becomes somewhat ludicrous to see the high hopes which even non-Orthodox Jews had placed—and which some continue to place—in a supreme Jewish ecclesiastical authority convening in Zion. As though such a body were to have intrinsic authority over Jews outside of its domain! As though such a body could even be aware of the practical problems of Jewish living in places far removed from its ken! And as though the burning problems of modern Judaism were primarily of a legalistic nature, subject to a religious lawyer's solution!

Still, if the reconvened *sanhedrin* did not materialize, there are other institutions which invest, or try to invest, the State of Israel with the aura of a "Spiritual Center," in a religious sense, for world Jewry. There is, for example, the institution of the Chief Rabbinate, an heirloom of the British Mandate of Palestine, and in itself of dubious roots within the Jewish tradition. The Chief Rabbinate is housed in a magnificent structure in Jerusalem; and, as he let it be known during the visit of the Pope to Israel in January 1964, the Israeli Sepharadi Chief Rabbi considers himself to be every inch the Jewish counterpart of the Roman Catholic Pope! Happily, this evaluation of the office is not generally shared even in Orthodox Jewish circles.

In fact, one seriously doubts whether the true heirs of Pharisaic-Rabbinic Judaism, some of whom are still to be found within the ranks of Orthodoxy, would even welcome the comparison between the Chief Rabbinate and the Papacy. The rabbinical degree is a testimony of its holder's proficiency in Jewish law and lore. It confers no priestly status upon the rabbi, who, technically, remains a layman. What authority he enjoys comes to him on account of the reputation he has acquired among those who voluntarily submit to his rulings. The Papacy, on the other hand, is not only based upon a strict hierarchical system; but the Pope is considered to be nothing less than Christ's representative on earth! Where Orthodox rabbis of an extremist hue play at popery, they merely prove that "assimilation" is by no means confined to those of lax ritual practice who have chosen as their domicile countries other than Israel.

Historically speaking, the whole concept of a "Spiritual Center" for religious guidance, which has to be located in one definite spot on earth, lacks all foundation as far as post-Biblical Judaism is concerned. There were times when

Palestine did serve as such a center. There were other times when Palestine was overshadowed by other centers. There even were times when Palestine itself had to be spiritually revitalized by the emissaries of the other centers.

In the Rabbinic period, with the decline of the Palestinian academies, the Babylonian academies came into ascendancy. So much so, in fact, that Rab Judah bar Ezekiel (b. *Kethuboth* 111b) expressly prohibited his disciples to go to Palestine for study purposes. Later, North Africa became a spiritual center. Then it was the turn of Spain. Other spiritual centers were to flourish in the Rhineland, once the French and German Jews had made themselves independent of the Babylonian academies. Later centers were to be established in Poland and in Lithuania. In more modern times, Germany became a spiritual center for world Jewry. It was there that the modern religious movements in Judaism had their origin: Reform Judaism, Conservative Judaism, and Modern Orthodoxy. It was there that the modern scientific study of Judaism (*Wissenschaft des Judentums*) was cultivated. After the catastrophe marking the end of European Jewry, the spiritual center of world Jewry shifted to the United States of America, with its five and a half million Jews, and its well-endowed institutions for Jewish scholarship and philanthropy. And another spiritual center might well be in the making in the State of Israel.

What makes a place a Jewish spiritual center? Simply, the opportunities afforded there for higher Jewish studies, and the presence there of one or more scholars of high repute whose advice and spiritual guidance are sought by communities far beyond the local one. When Rashi opened his academy in the French city of Troyes, in the eleventh century, and recognized authorities in Jewish law of other communities turned to Rashi for guidance, Troyes became a Jewish spiritual center. When Maimonides, in the twelfth century, resided in Egypt, and Jews from as far afield as Yemen, on the one hand, and the Provence, on the other, turned to him for decisions in matters legal and theological, the presence of Maimonides turned Egypt into a spiritual center for world Jewry. And when students from Hungary and Poland, England and the United States, flocked to the academies of higher Jewish learning in Germany, then Germany, too, became such a spiritual center.

There is no doubt that the State of Israel, likewise, has the potential of becoming a spiritual center in terms of this definition. Whether it will be *a* center, or *the* center, will depend upon the fate of the Jewish communities elsewhere. Certainly, the proclamation of Israel as *the* center implies a gloomy prognosis for the fate of other centers of Jewish learning, one which will not be cherished by any but the most doctrinaire political Zionist.

The pursuit of higher Jewish studies within a Hebrew-speaking environment, one in which a thorough knowledge of the contents of the Bible, if not always of its message, can be taken for granted, holds out great promise, and is sure to attract—and is already attracting—students from all over the world. The presence of world-famous authorities in the various disciplines of Judaic studies is another point in Israel's favor, supporting its claim to be a spiritual center.

But there is more to being a spiritual center than the provision of academic facilities. True, Judaism insists upon academic competence, on a mastery of the sources, as a prerequisite of spiritual leadership. Yet a knowledge of the sources is not enough. There must also be an application of that knowledge to the daily problems of Jewish living.

Even in earlier ages, when the answers to the problems of Jewish living were primarily sought in the legal realm, a knowledge of environmental factors and circumstances was an absolute prerequisite. That is why the literature of Rabbinic *responsa* is such an invaluable source for the study of Jewish history. The original questions, which were published alongside the legal answers, supply the kind of environmental background without which an adequate answer could not have been given. Today the basic problems of Jewish living are not primarily of a legalistic nature. Rather do they arise out of the philosophical and theological currents and crosscurrents affecting the orientation of the Jew in the particular environment in which he may be living. This may be on an abstract level. More concretely, a detailed knowledge of the environmental factors is essential when practical questions arise in connection with Jewish education, Sabbath and festival observance, not to mention the thorny problem of mixed marriages and intermarriages. For a spiritual center in the State of Israel to come to grips with such problems it would have to possess a knowledge of local circumstances even greater than that of the local experts. For it to have this kind of knowledge would be most unlikely. But if it does not do so, then it could not be appealed to as a source of guidance for the far-flung religious communities of Jews. Under the circumstances, the American Jew is more likely to find answers to his problems of Jewish living right within the borders of the United States than among the scholars and experts living in a different culture and environment.

Moreover, for real spiritual leadership more than expertise in the traditional sources of Jewish law and lore is required. More even than a thorough familiarity with the environment whence the request for guidance comes. There must also be a religious orientation on the part of the guide, an awareness of the lasting spiritual values and implications of the sources he has mastered.

Conceivably there could be gathered in Jerusalem an august body of scholars who, among them, have complete mastery of the whole range of Jewish literature, Biblical, Rabbinical, philosophical, historical, and mystical. But, unless such scholars also have a live interest in applying their knowledge to the solution of today's problems, what they have to offer will remain a mere preliminary step to the real spiritual guidance which is being sought. To date

there has not been much evidence which would indicate
that the world's experts in Jewish sources residing in Zion
have utilized their knowledge of those sources in a concentrated endeavor at a revitalization of Jewish faith and
living. Academic pursuits and religious reform are being
kept strictly separate. Perhaps it has to be so. The representatives of a medieval form of Judaism are still dominating
the religious scene in the State of Israel; and the acade-
micians may well feel that their freedom of scientific inquiry
already represents a gain which should not be endangered
by provoking the clericalists in the area of present-day religious polemics.

All this is perfectly understandable, and our sympathy
may legitimately be elicited by such growing pains of a
young country. But such understanding and sympathy on
our part can, at best, lead to the hope that, one day in the
future, the State of Israel may become one of the spiritual
centers of world Jewry. That, at this moment, it is already,
not just *a* center, but *the* "Spiritual Center" is an assertion
which goes beyond the innocent dreams of wish-fulfilment.
It is sheer deception.

At the beginning of this chapter, when we spoke about
the possible secular and religious meanings of the phrase,
"Spiritual Center," we also left open the possibility that
the phrase might refer to a combination of the two. It is
in this latter sense that many American Jews do, in fact,
look upon the "Spiritual Center" in Zion. Not being particularly interested in modern Hebrew literature, and not really
expecting Jerusalem to furnish detailed guidance for their
day-to-day religious living, they still feel that Judaism itself
will come to its maximum flowering within an environment
which is almost 100 per cent Jewish. Within such an environment, it is being claimed, Judaism will experience a rebirth.
If, in past generations, Judaism has suffered by many
accretions due to Ghetto existence, it will divest itself of
them in a sovereign Jewish State, and it will acquire a

natural vibrance and vitality which cannot help but be ultimately reflected in the kind of Judaism maintained outside the Jewish State.

What realistic grounds are there for such expectations? There is, for example, the sense of achievement which comes from the successful draining of swamps, and from "making the desert bloom," coupled as that sense is with an awareness of all this being "one's own work." The absence of anti-Semitism and racial or religious discrimination (at any rate, as practiced by the non-Jew) leads to the feeling that there is no part of your being which you need to soft-pedal or to hide. The sense of Jews defending themselves with guns, repelling the superior forces of the attackers, provides a welcome antidote to the events of recent history, made so well-known during the Eichmann trial, in which Jews figured as the passive victims of diabolical forces. All of these are ingredients which go into the psychological makeup of the Israeli; and that image of the "free Jew," transmitted to the Diaspora through such channels as Leon Uris' book (and film), *Exodus,* finds a ready response in the hearts of those Jews in the Diaspora who, for one reason or another, are ill-adjusted to their own environment.

To have the Jewish Sabbath and the Jewish festivals recognized as the legal days of rest prevents the kind of economic problems which observant Jews constantly face beyond the borders of Israel. (The fact that the clericalists are also able to dictate to the nonobservant the precise form which public observance of Sabbath and festivals has to take, is another problem.)

It is also true that, within Israel's agricultural setting, aspects of the Jewish festivals, which were largely ignored through the centuries, can again be emphasized. Rabbinic Judaism celebrated Passover primarily as a commemoration of God's redemptive acts in the Exodus from Egypt. Pentecost was the Feast of Divine Revelation. Tabernacles was made to express the faith in God's Providence. Yet, originally, the Biblical Pilgrim Festivals were agricultural festivals, expressing harvest joy and gratitude for first fruits. It is this original aspect of the festivals which has been revived in Israel, though not necessarily always within the original theistic setting, and often to the utter disregard of the spiritual meaning which was the foundation of the Rabbinic reinterpretation of those festivals. Occasions like Hanukkah and Purim, "minor festivals" of the traditional Jewish year, have become major events in the year of the Israeli, whereas the fifteenth day of the Hebrew month of Shevat, little more than a rubric in the traditional calendar, finds all the school children of the State of Israel engaged in a joyous tree-planting ceremony.

This has become possible by linking again the heritage of Judaism with the land in which it originated. The land, or rather *The* Land (for, when the Israeli uses the Hebrew word for "land" with the definite article, he means the State of Israel), has a *mystique* all its own. It is a *mystique* compounded of historical memories, pietistic associations, messianic dreams, and pride in recent achievements. Such a *mystique* is not amenable to cool clinical analysis. But, where it is shared by Jews in the Diaspora, belief in the State of Israel as Jewry's "Spiritual Center" becomes both a possibility and a necessity—regardless of whether or not the facts themselves warrant such a belief.

The *mystique* may not be amenable to complete analysis, but its historical origin can be described, and should be described, if only to clarify the position of those Jews who are unable to share it.

Whatever modern Jews may feel about the separation of Church and State, there can be no doubt that the thought of such a separation was completely alien to the Hebrew Bible. On the contrary, the Hebrew Bible itself is, at one and the same time, both the record of God's Revelation and the Constitution of the ancient Hebrew Commonwealth. The Biblical concept of the "Promised Land" was more than the concept of a haven of refuge for a horde of liberated Hebrew slaves from Egypt. Between the Exodus from Egypt and the Entry into the Promised Land there was the Revelation at Sinai, there was God's Covenant with Israel, making Israel "a kingdom of priests and a holy nation." It has frequently been noted that, whereas in Christianity, God's Covenant is with the saved individual, the Covenant in Judaism is with the redeemed *people*.

Biblical Israel, God's "chosen people," was to be a model society, its political no less than its cultic life was to be lived with reference to the Law of God. But model societies cannot exist in a geographical vacuum. They need a territory on which to establish themselves. And, according to the Bible, Palestine was to serve as that territory. It was the land which the Lord swore to the Patriarchs to give unto their descendants. Yet it was given only conditionally. If Israel abides by the terms of the Covenant, the land will be theirs. If Israel breaks the terms of the Covenant, then the land will "spew them out." This model society on Palestinian soil was not to exist for Israel's benefit alone. At the end of the historical process, according to the second chapter of the Book of Isaiah, all nations were to turn to it, saying: "Come ye, and let us go up to the mountain of the Lord, to the house of the God of Jacob. And He will teach us of His ways; and we shall walk in His paths. For out of Zion shall go forth instruction, and the word of the Lord from Jerusalem."

History and its messianic redemption were thus linked to the soil of Palestine. Whatever, therefore, took place there on the historical level had its true significance in the religious realm—both positively and negatively. National prosperity was seen in terms of religious obedience, and national defeat as the direct result of religious unfaithfulness. The disappearance of the Northern Kingdom of Israel, in 722 B.C.E., was regarded as the consequence of straying after strange gods. The destruction of the Southern Kingdom of Judah,

in 586 B.C.E., was likewise interpreted as punishment for
the sins committed by the people, the Babylonian Exile
being a period of expiation.

The Hebrew Bible ends with the edict of Cyrus permit-
ting the exiles' return to Palestine. Only a minority of the
exiles availed themselves of this opportunity. Those who
did laid the foundations of a new Jewish Commonwealth
in Palestine. But the Second Commonwealth was not to
last much longer than the first. It, too, ultimately was destroyed, and this second destruction was described by the
Rabbis of the Talmud, just like the Biblical writers' description of the first destruction, as a consequence of Israel's
sins. The Rabbis were no less aware than the Biblical writers
of the conditional nature of Israel's possession of the Promised
Land. "On account of our sins," they prayed, and Orthodox
Jews pray to this day, "we were exiled from our land, and
removed from our soil."

Rabbinic Judaism, for its part, for all of its bemoaning
of Israel's being "in exile," was able to fashion a faith and
a way of life which were independent of Jewish occupancy
of Palestinian territory. It distinguished between the "commandments dependent upon the Land" and the commandments not so dependent, a distinction which more or less
separated the political components of Scripture from the
purely religious ones. Only the latter were now deemed to
be binding upon the Jew. The former were temporarily
suspended.

Suspended, but not abolished! For, to the Rabbis, the
Bible, even in its territorially bound components, was the
Word of God. Dispensing with the observance of the "commandments dependent upon the Land" was, in spite of
its practicality, merely a makeshift arrangement. The Rabbis
might have found in prayer, in study, and in charity adequate substitutes for the sacrificial cult of the Jerusalem
Temple, and they have enabled generations of Jews to live
lives of piety without benefit of sacrifice and priesthood.

But sacrifice and priesthood were components, outstanding components, of the legal books of the Pentateuch, and the Pentateuch was deemed to be the Word of God for all time. Consequently, the Rabbis were longing for the day when the whole of the divine legislation would again be put into practice. They were, in other words, looking forward to, and praying for, the return of Israel to its old Promised Land, so that the divinely ordained cult could be resumed. The Biblical prophecies heralding the end of the Babylonian Exile were now applied to the end of the current exile, an exile which has turned out to last many times the traditional "seventy years" of its Babylonian prototype.

Deepening such Rabbinic considerations, the twelfth-century poet-philosopher Judah Halevi evolved a theory of Judaism which made the flowering of the Jewish spirit contingent upon the observance of the totality of the Biblical commandments (including those which were "dependent upon the Land"), and, consequently, upon the Jewish occupancy of Palestine. Giving expression to this thought both in his philosophical treatise and in his poetry, he has achieved the reputation of being the first Zionist. How he would have reacted to secularist Jewish nationalism would make for interesting speculation. At any rate, the fact remains that the type of thinking represented by Halevi was nourished by, and, in turn, fed, the romanticism and the *mystique* of the Land.

It is this type of thinking which, in many circles, prepared the ground for modern Zionism, which induces American Jews to think in terms of an Israeli "Spiritual Center," and which makes many an American Jew thrill at the sight of a travel poster, inviting him to visit "Israel—Land of the Bible." The connection between the Land and the Book is obvious. But, perhaps, the consequences of that connection were not always, and not uniformly, understood in a way which would limit the applicability of the Biblical faith to certain geographical boundaries. After all, according to the

Biblical account itself, God's Revelation to Moses and the Children of Israel took place, not within the boundaries of the ancient Jewish State, but in the wilderness of Sinai. This fact prompted one of the ancient Rabbis to ask, "Why was the Torah given in the wilderness?" And the answer he propounded was that, just as the wilderness, being no man's land, is free to all, so the words of the Torah are free to all the dwellers on earth, with no national entity entitled to lay exclusive claim to the possession of God's Word. (*Numbers Rabbah* 1:6.)

It is true, of course, that many of the early crucial stages in the drama of Jewish history were acted out upon Palestinian soil. But it is also true that Jewish life and thought have likewise flourished outside of Palestine—and that for a period of longer duration than the one which measures the days of the First and Second Jewish Commonwealths. The persecution to which Jews were subjected during so many centuries may account for the feeling of being "in exile" which animates so much of traditional Jewish literature, and it undoubtedly is responsible for much of the romanticism with which Jews endowed the memories of, and the hopes for, the Holy Land. But, in terms of the realities of Jewish achievement, it would be hard to maintain that the Babylonian Rabbis were less intensely Jewish than the contemporaries of King David, or that Maimonides, in Spain and Egypt, was less able to develop his full spiritual potential than the contemporaries of Ezra and Nehemiah in Palestine. In terms of the realities of Jewish achievement, the Palestine-centered philosophy of Jewish living, whether it be that of the medieval Judah Halevi, or that of the modern secularist Zionist, will be found wanting on several counts.

And not only in terms of the realities. Theologically, too, such a philosophy leaves much to be desired. Linking gods, cults, and territories is no particular Jewish achievement. That was the pattern of ancient paganism. It may well be that, for a time, ancient Israel adopted the same pattern.

But therein ancient Israel did not excel her neighbors. It was precisely the fact that Israel's Prophets learned to look beyond the national horizon, and realized that the God of Israel could be adored "from the rising of the sun unto the going down thereof," which marked the unique contribution of Israel's Prophetic religion. To maintain, after all this, that Israel's faith is for all time bound up with a certain territory, that geography is the determining factor in living one's life according to the Will of God—to maintain that amounts to nothing less than a retrogression to the territorial gods of ancient paganism, to a denial of the Prophetic claim (Malachi 1:5) that "God is great beyond the borders of Israel!"

For the Jew who lived in the narrow Ghetto lane, a Jewish State in Palestine represented a vision of breadth and enlargement. But, for the Jew who had stepped out of the Ghetto, the thought of a Jewish restoration to Palestine itself conveyed an undesirable limitation and confinement. That is why, on the one hand, the Jewish Middle Ages are dominated by the thoughts of Exile and Restoration, and why, on the other hand, the Jewish Reformers of the nineteenth century, children of the era of Emancipation, singled out the universalistic elements of Israel's faith as the *raison d'être* for Israel's continued existence in the four corners of the earth.

They did not deny that, at one time, their ancestors led a corporate kind of existence on the soil of the Holy Land. On the contrary, they maintained that that form of existence was an integral part of God's plan for the training of His "kingdom of priests and holy people." But they refused to envisage a future which would be identical with the past. They not only asserted that Israel had outgrown the Palestinian phase of its development, but they also saw in the historical events which led to the separation of Land and People the workings of that God of History Who had destined His Chosen People for a fate and a mission other

than those of nations whose spiritual life is bounded by their
geographical borders.

The Jews of Eastern Europe who did not enjoy the bene-
fits of Emancipation, and the Zionist theoreticians who arose
in their midst, were never able to appreciate this particular
reading of the facts of Jewish history. And the catastrophic
events, which, in our century, have so painfully refuted the
easy optimism of the nineteenth century, are now generally
understood to have likewise disproved the philosophy of
Jewish existence which the early Reformers propounded. Yet
that philosophy, though made popular by the conditions
created by the Emancipation, is not itself dependent upon
those conditions. Progress may not be quite as automatic as
people thought in the nineteenth century. The civil rights
of the Jew may be less assured, at any given moment, in
one country than they are in another. But the *destiny* of the
Jew, as distinct from his temporary welfare, is something
which can only be seen *sub specie aeternitatis*. And from the
perspective which classical Reform Judaism took of Jewish
destiny as a whole, Jewish history will always be read as
the development which led from clan to nation, and from
nation to world-wide religious community.

There will undoubtedly always be those who prefer a
different perspective, a view of the Jews which sees them
as a nation "like all the other nations," which regards the
first two millennia of the Common Era as the time when
that nation was "in exile," and which looks forward to the
"ingathering of the exiles" in the restored "homeland."
Such a view could certainly be supported by many quota-
tions from Jewish literature. But the perseverance of such
a view neither proves its truth nor disproves the view propounded by the pioneers of Reform Judaism. Only the God
of History Himself is in a position to give a verdict.

In the meantime, the proponents of both views will have
to learn to accept the fact of each other's existence. While
their hopes for the future may diverge, they are bound by a

common respect for the past. Both revere the Land of Israel as the "cradle of our faith." But, while one group longs to return to that "cradle," to Israel's childhood, the other has already learned that maturity implies the recognition that one has outgrown his cradle, that the days of childhood will never return again. The former group may indeed be impressed by the claim that the State of Israel is the Jew's "Spiritual Center," although, as we have noted, it is a claim which, even for that group, is not without its inner contradictions and difficulties. But, for the latter group, the claim itself sounds like a mere echo from a distant past, beyond recovery.

CHAPTER FOUR

Challenge to American Judaism

One might have supposed that the point of view represented in the preceding pages would be the one adopted by the majority of American Jews, and certainly by the official religious institutions of American Judaism. Both logic and enlightened self-interest would seem to militate against the acceptance of the philosophy of Jewish nationalism by American Jews, at least by those of them who have decided not to pull up their American roots in order to emigrate to the State of Israel. And that includes the vast majority of Jews in America. Nor would one expect the responsible leadership of American Jewish religious institutions to ignore the reasons, both historical and theological, which have led us to the repudiation of the claim that the State of Israel is *the* "Spiritual Center" for Jews the world over.

In point of fact, however, neither logic nor self-interest, neither history nor theology, have been persuasive enough to prevent the Zionist coloration of American Jewish life. Of course, the number of American Jews who actually leave for the State of Israel (and do not return) is minimal enough. There are a few whose deep ideological commitment to Zionism makes it impossible for them to stop short of *aliyah* (immigration to Israel). There are a few youngsters, as there always are among all peoples and countries, who seek their self-fulfilment beyond the seas. There are those who have been failures, socially and professionally, and who seek the solution to their problems in the Promised Land. And then there are those few elderly people, mostly of East European antecedents, who find that their Social Security dollar stretches further beyond the borders of the United States. And, if the choice is between Mexico and Israel, the memories of their childhood milieu tip the scales in favor of the latter. But the numbers involved in all of those categories represent no significant depletion of the Jewish population of the United States. They are, in fact, so minimal that the absence of any large-scale American Jewish immigration to Israel provides a continuous headache for the government of the State of Israel and for Zionist officialdom.

If we can nevertheless speak of the Zionist coloration of American Jewish life, it is because, in their thinking and in their pronouncements, American Jews act as though they had accepted the basic premises of the Zionist philosophy. Without, in any way, being negligent of their obligations to the United States, many American Jews have a tendency of also regarding the State of Israel as "their" country. They take considerable pride in Israel's achievements, and they feel called upon to "defend" the acts of the Israeli government, whatever they may be, before the bar of public opinion. "A non-Zionist may or may not come to the moral defense of Israel at a juncture in international politics when Israel's position may be for the time being quite unpopular with the state of which he is a citizen; a Zionist cannot do otherwise than come to the moral defense of Israel, endeavoring to enlighten, explain and overcome misunderstandings, no matter how unpopular that role may be." (Israel Goldstein, *Transition Years*. Jersusalem, Rubin Mass, 1962, page 77.) The distinction made between popularity and unpopularity seems to leave no room for that other, and more basic, distinction between right and wrong. American Jews, or at least their vocal Zionist elements, tend to assume that the State of Israel is always in the right.

Similarly, although the majority of them are quite unable to read a Hebrew book, American Jews, by and large, take it for granted that the culture produced in the State of Israel is "Jewish culture," and, therefore, their culture, too. A Hanukkah candlestick, or a silken prayer-shawl, bearing the imprint "Made in Israel" will, whatever their artistic and esthetic merits, be preferred to the local products. All this is innocent enough. It assumes more serious proportions once the American Jew begins to feel spiritually and religiously inferior to the Jew in Israel. Then he starts educating his children (or, rather, lets the Zionist schools do the educating for him) in the doctrine that the Judaism of the Diaspora is a kind of second-class Judaism, and that a "full Jewish life" can only be led in the State of Israel. And if, at a synagogal Hebrew and Religious School, an Israeli should apply for a teaching post (and, peculiarly enough, there seem to be quite a few Israelis around, in the United States!), then he can be sure that few, if any, inquiries will be made as to his religious views (which, in the majority of cases, are either negative or nonexistent); his country of origin alone will be considered sufficient qualification for imparting a knowledge of Judaism and its sacred texts to the children of American Jews.

Often such a teacher will find textbooks as though made to order, textbooks, appearing under the imprint of American Jewish religious organizations, which aim at creating a closer bond between the American Jewish child and the life being lived in the State of Israel. Nor are American Jewish educators averse to utilizing the propaganda literature, or even the personnel, made available by agencies of the Israeli government or the Zionist Organization.

As for the public image projected by American Jewish life, the focal point of organized Jewish activity, it may safely be asserted that it is being furnished by the functions held in connection with the State of Israel. United Jewish Appeal dinners, Bonds for Israel rallies, Hadassah fashion shows, and the like, make up the official calendar of Jewish life in America.

We have already had occasion to note that few American Jews are aware of the political implications of their supposedly philanthropic gifts. The fact remains that, wittingly or unwittingly, American Jews are playing into the hands of the Zionists. At the meeting of the Zionist General Council, held in Jerusalem, in March, 1964, Israel's Prime Minister, Mr. Levi Eshkol, speaking about the renewed Zionist campaign "to conquer the communities," promised his government's "every moral and political support. And if it should happen that the Movement and the Jewish people cannot bear the material burden alone, the Government will also lend a hand here—if asked, and to the limits of its capacity." (*The Jerusalem Post,* March 17, 1964, page 1.)

In all but the final step, that of inducing the Jews of America to settle in Israel, the campaign of "conquering" the American Jewish community has undoubtedly had more success already than might be adduced from the urgent tones with which it is currently being renewed.

American Judaism has not always been like this. It became that way only from the nineteen-thirties on. Obviously, it has responded to certain stimuli which had not been present before then. And it is not difficult to see to what American Judaism has been responding.

There was, first of all, the rising tide of anti-Semitism in Europe, culminating in the destruction of six million European Jews during World War II. There was hardly a Jewish family in the United States which did not lose one or more relatives, near or distant, in this slaughter. Apart from certain doubts which this catastrophe inevitably raised about the universal feasibility of Jewish Emancipation, it also produced psychological guilt feelings. My brothers are being killed in Europe, and I lead the life of luxury in America! Such a state of mind made for an easy acceptance of Zionist claims, particularly when the latter were presented as appeals for aid to the remnant which remained of European Jewry, and as blueprints for a "homeland" the very existence of which would make it impossible for the tragic events of Europe to be repeated in the future.

A second factor to be reckoned with is the preponderance of Jews from East European backgrounds. Such Jews immigrated into the United States in vast numbers at the turn of the century. Prior to their arrival, the dominant form of Judaism in the United States had been fashioned by Jews of German provenance. The difference between the German and the East European Jews was more than one of geographical background. The Jews of Germany had already been permitted to leave the Ghetto before they embarked for America. They had already been given an opportunity to absorb, and to participate in, Western culture. Linguistically and culturally they were Germans, and many of them maintained that culture even after they had become loyal citizens of the United States of America. To the extent to which they also asserted their "Jewishness," it was purely and simply a matter of their religious affiliation.

Not so the East European Jews who came to the freedom of America straight out of the oppressive Ghetto existence of Russia and Poland. They had never been emancipated. They had never been allowed to share in the culture of their environment. They did not come as Russians, or as Poles, of the Jewish faith. They came as Jews from Russia and Poland. The "Jewishness" they brought with them was not simply a matter of religious belief and practice. It was, rather, a whole complex of folkways and folk-feeling, of language and of mores, of cuisine and of literature. Indeed, what they brought with them was that whole syndrome which, in common parlance, passes for "Jewish culture," even though that culture is not shared by Jews of any other background.

The East European Jewish immigrants did not, at first, reshape the structure and the outlook of American Judaism.

They were poor; they eked out a pitiful living in "sweat-shops." Above all, they did not speak the language of the country. Their children, however, not only outnumbered the American Jews of German provenance, but, thanks to America's system of free education, they grew up with the same advantages and the same opportunities. In due course, the second and third generations of East European Jewish immigrants were to take their rightful place within the organizations and institutions of American Judaism, and to dominate them by sheer force of numbers.

It is easy to understand that Zionism has always found a more ready echo in the hearts of East European Jews than in those of their German brethren. Zionism spoke to their condition. Zionism operated with their concepts. And Zionism utilized their folk-feeling. In return, the families of East European origin identified their awareness of the Jewish heritage with the categories furnished by Zionist thought. In this way, an attachment to Jewish nationalism became part of the family tradition in those circles. To this must be added one further consideration. In their process of acclimatization to the American environment, the East European Jewish immigrants noticed that, without calling into question their American loyalties, American society recognized the existence of "hyphenated Americans," e.g., the Irish-American, the Italian-American, the German-American, etc. What, then, lay closer to hand than the concept of the Jewish-American? Of course, the Jewish-American was not altogether comparable to the other "hyphenated Americans." The latter came from such countries as Ireland, Italy, or Germany, while the Jewish-American did not come from a "Jewish" country—at least not within a memory stretching back to less than two thousand years. But, if there was no question of the American loyalties of the Irish-American who paraded down Fifth Avenue on St. Patrick's Day, it seemed logical to suppose that the support of Zionism would likewise fit into the over-all American pattern.

After all, America prided itself on being a pluralistic society!

When, therefore, the descendants of the East European Jewish immigrants, on account of their numbers, and on account of their rapid acclimatization, began to dominate the organizations and the institutions of American Judaism, they were instrumental in bringing about a climate of opinion in which Zionism was not only tolerated, but in which it was actually encouraged to flourish. This process may be studied in detail by looking at the history of the Jewish Welfare Funds, of B'nai B'rith, of the American Jewish Committee, of the Union of American Hebrew Congregations, and of Reform Judaism's Central Conference of American Rabbis.

Yet the factors we have so far adduced do not tell the complete story. Indeed, the most important factor involved in American Judaism's turn to Zionism still remains to be considered. And it is in connection with this factor that we see the true nature of the challenge which Zionism presents to American Judaism. Zionism, for many of its adherents, is a substitute religion; and it flourishes precisely because the real religion which it has come to replace is weak and colorless, and bypasses the real needs of the people.

Orthodox Judaism in America has for some two generations suffered from an inability to communicate, to make itself known to Jews born and educated in the United States. There were, of course, exceptions. But, by and large, in the mind of the people, Orthodox Judaism was identified with the life and the mores of the "old country." The rabbis spoke Yiddish. Many of them sported the attire of Eastern Europe. And the system of religious education, although hardly as intensive as it used to be in Russia and Poland, was but a continuation and adaptation of the East European kind. The contrasts between it and the secular education to which the youngsters were exposed did not help in the creation of a healthy synthesis. Perhaps even worse was the attitude of suspicion with which the Orthodox rabbinate confronted everything on the American scene which did not have its counterpart in the Jewish environment of Eastern Europe. It goes without saying that there was no coming to terms with the changed conditions of life, and of thought. The result was a large-scale turning away from Orthodoxy, either as a consciously chosen path of rebellion, or as a matter of indifferent drifting.

Happily, there has, of late, been a change for the better. A generation of English-speaking Orthodox rabbis, trained in the United States, backed by an increasing number of intelligent and devoted laymen, is well on the way to making Orthodox Judaism intellectually respectable. We see an Orthodoxy which endeavors to combine strict adherence to the traditional Jewish law with a full participation in the culture, the literature, the philosophy, and the science of the Western tradition. Without departing from the norms laid down in the ritual codes, this Orthodoxy does not feel itself tied to the externals acquired during Ghetto existence, and it acknowledges the right of esthetics to voice its claim.

Such a type of Orthodoxy, as we said, may yet succeed in establishing itself on American soil—particularly since this modern type of Orthodoxy has, within recent years, made vast strides in creating an ever widening network of Jewish day schools. But, whether it will succeed or not, this type of Orthodoxy is a relatively new phenomenon on the American Jewish scene. It was not readily available a generation or two ago, at a time when its availability might have prevented the loosening of religious ties.

Where religious Orthodoxy refused to grapple with the intellectual problems posed by the twentieth century, Zionism presented itself as a made-to-order substitute religion. Its rewriting of Jewish history in secularist-nationalist terms enabled the Jew to bypass the metaphysics of "sacred history," and to maintain a link with the ancestral past in spite of his abandonment of ancestral presuppositions.

The step into the American twentieth century, which

Orthodoxy refused to take at all, Reform Judaism gloried in taking, and that in seven-league boots. With a relentless logic, "classical" Reform Judaism, in its endeavor to be absolutely "rational," proceeded to banish every element of the "irrational" from Judaism. Even the idea of the Deity retained precious little of the "numinous." If Reform started by removing from the liturgy those sections in which one no longer "believed" (e.g., the personal Messiah, the Return to Zion, the Restoration of the sacrificial cult, the Resurrection of the dead, the angels), it did not take too long for Reform to find itself caught in the thicket of an even more thorny liturgical problem: the value of prayer itself, the existence of a God "Who hears prayers." For, if you make your commitment to God dependent upon the outcome of your reasoning, there is at least a tacit admission that it is possible for your reasoning to take a different course and lead you to an entirely different destination. If you insist, as "classical" Reform Judaism did, that *everything* in religion is meant to serve ethical needs, it will not be long before upholders of an ethical way of life start claiming that they can have their ethics without the religion. Felix Adler, who began by studying for the Reform rabbinate, and who became the founder of the Ethical Culture Movement, is a case in point.

If you deny the relevance of *halakhah* (the life-regimen of Torah law), as "classical" Reform Judaism did deny it, and make religious observance entirely dependent on the taste of the individual and the whim of the moment, the very factors which made Israel of old a *religious* community, rather than a secular nation, will have been cast aside.

If you sermonize at length on how the ancient Prophets fulminated against Temple worship in Jerusalem and in Beth-El, and "classical" Reform Judaism did so sermonize, then one day the congregations begin to wonder how important Temple worship in New York or in Cincinnati can be in the sight of God. And why have religious services at all, if God is best worshiped in the heart of man and served by the moral deed!

Although, within recent years, some of the younger theologians within the Reform movement have shown themselves fully aware of these problems, and have tried to come to terms with them by again taking seriously such rather neglected concepts as Revelation and the Covenant, there seems to have been little recognition, in earlier phases of Reform Judaism, of the paradoxes which it harbored. These paradoxes might sooner or later have brought about the internal collapse of Reform Judaism as an institutional religion. But, in the nick of time, Reform Judaism discovered Jewish "peoplehood." And, in 1937, the Central Conference of American Rabbis not only recognized "in the group-loyalty of Jews who have become estranged from our religious tradition a bond which still unites them with us," but also proclaimed the upbuilding of a Jewish Homeland in Palestine as a religious duty for Reform Jews.

In short, hanging on to the Zionist lifeline was seen as Reform Judaism's salvation just when it came dangerously close to the abyss of its own theological deficiencies. It is not surprising, however, that many American Jews find it possible to take their Zionism without the trappings of a religious "denomination." This is particularly the case in the absence of any definite *religious* program which Reform Judaism, for quite some time, has had to offer its adherents. The battles of the last century have been won, and putting the hat on, or taking it off, is not an issue which can satisfy modern religious craving.

If Reform Judaism came around to an affirmation of Jewish "peoplehood" in the nineteen-thirties, this affirmation had always been the cornerstone of Conservative Judaism. Sociologically, Conservative Judaism has been described as "the Reform Judaism of the East European immigrant." Theologically, it has always shied away from definitions, and, in terms of religious observance, it has always afforded a sufficient degree of flexibility to make its "right-wing" congregations indistinguishable from "left-wing" Orthodoxy, and its "left-wing" congregations practically identical with "right-wing" Reform. But Conservative Judaism has always insisted on the centrality of Jewish "peoplehood," on the importance of the Hebrew language, on the building of a Jewish State, and on ritual observance as a token of Jewish self-identification. That, within this climate of opinion, Zionism has always found its most fertile soil goes without saying. It is, therefore, all the more remarkable (and, perhaps, a straw in the wind?) that, when it was invited to join the World Zionist Organization as a body, some years ago, the Conservative United Synagogue of America refused to do so.

What is there by implication in Conservative Judaism is spelled out in great detail in Reconstructionism. Seeing religion as only one part of a total "Jewish civilization," Reconstructionism's coat of arms locates the State of Israel in the very center of things. Belief in the personal God has been given up. (God is a process.) Belief in the divine election of the People of Israel is emphatically rejected. But customs and ceremonies are definitely encouraged—as Jewish "folkways."

This, in brief, and not taking into account some notable exceptions, is the picture of organized Jewish religious life in the United States. All spiritual roads seem to lead to Zion. So far, in our century, religious Judaism has made little more than a beginning in addressing itself to the American Jew in the "here and now." It has not, again with some exceptions, spoken to him very much about the God of Abraham, Isaac, and Jacob. It has not widely discussed with him the problem of Revelation, apart from either a dogmatic insistence upon the literal truth of the Biblical account, or an equally dogmatic assertion that the "findings of modern Biblical scholarship" have solved the problem of Revelation—negatively. It has not fundamentally come to terms with prayer, apart from creating the kind of esthetic setting within which true prayer *could* be possible. It has not really delved into the question of Jewish identity, in terms of membership in a "covenant community." It has always been too ready to identify the sum-total of the millennial Jewish tradition with the latest liberal political platforms and with the most fashionable fads in popular philosophy and psychiatry.

What wonder, then, that, where the riddle of Jewish existence is seriously faced and deeply felt, all eyes turn longingly toward Jerusalem! What wonder that, without offering too much resistance, American Jews meekly accept the role assigned to them by classical Zionism, that of Jews unable to "live a full Jewish life!" What wonder that Zion is expected to provide what America has failed to furnish!

If Zion were only in a position to provide! But this is the real tragedy of the situation: that, as our previous chapters have endeavored to show, the Torah is not coming forth out of Zion, nor the Word of the Lord from Jerusalem. Spiritually, to say the least, the Jews in the State of Israel are not more favored than their brethren in America. Nor, for that matter, is Zion's potential greater than that of the United States. On the contrary, with all of the aspects of Jewish life in America, which are in dire need of improvement, Jews in the United States have the kind of material resources which are the envy of the Israelis, resources which can support the institutions necessary for a flourishing Jewish life. And they have the freedom in which to develop them, a freedom not possessed by the Israelis—the freedom from government interference in religious affairs.

Under the circumstances, the challenge presented to American Judaism by the State of Israel is a spurious challenge; and nobody who knows the true state of affairs in Israel can, with any degree of honesty, hold up Israeli religious life as something worthy of imitation elsewhere; let alone as something to attract large-scale immigration from the United States. And yet, there remains a twofold challenge which must be faced, if we are to do justice to all of the implications of the present situation.

If, instead of being promised heaven on earth in the State of Israel, American Jews were told of the actual conditions prevailing there, it is not at all unlikely that there will be found among American Jews those who would want to contribute their share in laying the foundations of what, one day, might become an important spiritual center. Just as the Palestinian deserts and swamps attracted the pioneers who turned them into habitable regions, so the oppressive religious climate of the State of Israel and the spiritual wastelands might attract those who are willing to help in the creation of a healthier religious climate and in the development of a more adequate Jewish way of life. Such a challenge will not necessarily appeal to the vast majority of American Jewish youth, any more than the missionary needs of the various Christian churches are ever completely met. But it is an opportunity for service which should not be lost sight of, and which should have as much claim on our attention as other worthy schemes, such as the Peace Corps.

That is the first part of the challenge. The second part lies closer to home. If we are already reckoning with the possibility of helping in the creation of a flourishing Jewish life in a foreign country, it stands to reason that we cannot, and we must not, be blind to the needs of our own country. Zionists are in the habit of referring to Jews living outside of the State of Israel as living "in exile." Non-Zionist Jews, enjoying the freedom of the United States and of other free countries, have been known to reject the concept of "exile" most emphatically. This disagreement is liable to be with us for quite some time to come. It is a disagreement which will not be resolved as long as it is based on either an unconscious misunderstanding or on a wilful distortion of the concept of "exile." As this writer sees it, the Jews of America do indeed live "in exile," and the sooner they recognize it, the more adequately they will be able to deal with the situation. But as true as it is that the Jews of America are living "in exile," so is it true that the Jews of the State of Israel are living "in exile," too. Basic to our understanding of the concept of "exile" is an awareness of the long history of the evolution of this concept—a concept which has implications both of a geographical and of a temporal nature.

The concept of "exile" entered the Jewish world of thought when, in the sixth century B.C.E., the Kingdom of Judah was destroyed by the Babylonians, and when many of its inhabitants were led into captivity. Owing to the teachings of the Hebrew Prophets, this course of events was not understood in terms of power politics, but rather as divine punishment meted out for disobedience of the Law of God. With this awareness of the punitive nature of historical reality went the hope that the period of punishment will be terminated when the sin has been expiated, and that God would "restore the captivity of Zion." This hope was indeed fulfilled when Cyrus gave permission to the Jewish exiles to return to Palestine, and when, in due course, the Second Jewish Commonwealth was founded, and the Jerusalem Temple was rebuilt. "Exile," therefore, in spite of its religious meaning, was basically a geographical concept, i.e., a people removed from its native soil. But, as such, the "Babylonian Exile" was deemed to have been terminated by the edict of Cyrus with which the Hebrew Bible concludes (II Chronicles 36:22-23.).

We have already had occasion to note that the majority of the Jews in the "Babylonian Captivity" did not avail themselves of this permission to return to Palestine. Moreover, during the days of the Second Temple an increasing number of Jews *voluntarily* left Palestine in order to settle throughout the Mediterranean world. It is important to realize that this exodus from Palestine was not forced upon the Jews by a foreign power, that it took place when there was an independent Jewish State, when there was a Temple in Jerusalem, and, during the Hasmonean period, when an independent Jewish dynasty occupied the throne of Judaea. Those Jewish pioneers and settlers in the Hellenistic and Roman world were indeed bound by ties of kinship to their Palestinian brethren, and, on account of the Jerusalem Temple, to which they made frequent pilgrimages, they did see in Palestine the spiritual center of their faith. It was, after all, "the place which the Lord had chosen to cause His Name to dwell there." Yet the fact remains that, toward the end of the days of the Second Temple, more Jews were actually living, and had chosen so to live, outside of Palestine than within the Jewish State itself. Such Jews were referred to, and referred to themselves, as living "in the Diaspora." The word "Diaspora" is Greek for "dispersion," and was descriptive of the wide geographical spread of the Jewish communities in the Mediterranean world. But it was also the word used by the Greek translation of the Bible to render the Hebrew word which more specifically means "exile." It goes without saying, however, that the painful connotation of "exile," exemplified by the "Babylonian Captivity," was hardly the connotation applicable to the many communities of Jews who voluntarily sought their fortunes elsewhere at a time when an independent Jewish State was in existence. "Diaspora," for them, was a purely geographical concept. It described the area of residence of the non-Palestinian Jews.

It is, of course, true that prayers written at that time express the hope for an "ingathering of the exiles." The Hebrew version of *Ecclesiasticus* (51:2, v-vii) contains the prayer: "Give thanks unto Him that gathereth the outcasts of Israel; for His mercy endureth forever. Give thanks unto Him that buildeth His city and His sanctuary; for His mercy endureth forever." Similarly, the *Psalms of Solomon* (8:33-35), probably dating from the middle of the first century B.C.E., plead: "Turn, O God, Thy tender mercy upon us, and have pity upon us; gather together the dispersed of Israel, with mercy and goodness; for Thy faithfulness is with us." But, seeing that at the time when those prayers were composed the Temple was actually in existence, and that the "outcasts" and the "dispersed of Israel" were emigrants from Palestine of their own free will, it seems more than likely that the Biblical imagery used in the prayers was more of an expression of the *spiritual* unity of Israel than a plea for the dissolution of the Diaspora.

This was to change, however, once the Second Jewish State was destroyed by the Romans in the year 70 C.E. Here, again, "exile" in its "Babylonian" connotation was felt to have come upon the Jews. The destruction of Temple and State was understood as divine punishment for a sinful people. And just as the hope of restoration accompanied the awareness of punishment in the sixth century B.C.E., so was a like hope to sustain the people now. The old prophecies promising an end to the "Babylonian Exile" were now applied to the anticipated end of the "Roman Exile." The Temple would be rebuilt, the Jews, forcefully expelled by the Romans from Palestine, would be restored to their homeland, and a king of the Davidic dynasty would again reign over them.

This new awareness of "exile" thus had both its political and its religious connotations. Religious, because the destruction of the Temple led to the cessation of the sacrificial cult, and because the loss of the land made inoperative a considerable portion of Biblical legislation. The totality of religious observance suffered a grievous diminution. Political, because, first under pagan Rome, and later under Christian Rome, the Jews were indeed subjected to suffering and persecution. "Exile," therefore, was both the *enforced* absence of Jews from Palestine, and the period in history preceding the messianic redemption. At this point of the evolution of the concept of "exile," we find it to be composed of political, religious, geographical, and temporal elements. All of those elements would disappear in the "days of the Messiah," the coming of which was the constant burden of fervent prayer. But what are "the days of the Messiah?" Here, Biblical prophecy and popular belief, dogmatic formulation and eschatological hope, presented a wide variety of expectations. Among them was the statement of the third-century Babylonian teacher, Samuel, codified nine centuries later by Maimonides, that "the only difference between this world and the days of the Messiah is the absence of the subjugation of the Jews to foreign kingdoms." (B. *Berakhoth* 34b, and *Hilkhoth Melakhim* 12:2.)

It was in line with this sentiment that the Reformers of the nineteenth century rejected the concept of "living in exile." Enforced ghetto existence, living at the periphery of society, that was one thing. But obtaining the rights of full citizenship was quite another. The Jews living as citizens of a modern state could not by any stretch of the imagination be considered as living "in subjugation to foreign kingdoms." And if, as Samuel and Maimonides had clearly stated, it was this "subjugation" which made the difference between "this world" and "the days of the Messiah," then the messianic era had obviously begun to dawn already, and the concept of "exile" had lost its validity.

With no less a show of logic than was employed by the early Reformers, the Zionists, after 1948, saw in the establishment of the State of Israel the end of "the subjugation of the Jews to foreign kingdoms." For them, too, the messianic era had dawned. But they continued to look upon the Jews not resident in the State of Israel as "living in exile"—thereby injecting the negative connotation of "exile" into the objectively valid description of "Diaspora." The latter, in the Zionist view, is not merely the geographical "dispersion" of the Jews throughout the world, but the undesirable state of "being in exile," a state of being which was left behind by those Jews who make the State of Israel their home.

It can be argued that neither the early Reformers nor the Zionists have done full justice to the criterion laid down by Samuel and Maimonides. Whatever may have been the situation in nineteenth-century Germany and America, more recent events in Jewish history have demonstrated all too clearly that, as far as the *totality* of Jews is concerned, "the subjugation to foreign kingdoms" had not come to an end. Similarly, however proud the modern Israeli may be of his Israeli citizenship, the precarious political situation of the State of Israel at this time would hardly qualify it to be regarded as the fulfilment of the messianic hopes cherished by Samuel in the third century, and by Maimonides in the twelfth.

But, quite apart from the legitimacy of the arguments used by both the early Reformers and by the Zionists, an even more basic criticism which may be leveled against them is the fact that, in their understanding of "exile" and messianic redemption, they concentrated on the *political* aspects of those concepts. As we have noted, the concept of "exile" as understood by the Rabbis after the destruction of Temple and State, in the year 70 C.E., included *religious* elements as well. Maimonides was aware of this. That is why his vision of the "days of the Messiah" included not only the political freedom of the Jews, but also the rebuilding of the Temple, and the restoration of the sacrificial service. (*Hilkhoth Melakhim* 11:1.)

Neither Maimonides nor, we may rightly assume, the Babylonian Samuel overlooked the religious aspects of the messianic fulfilment when they stressed the cessation of "subjugation to foreign kingdoms." Political independence was a precondition for the restoration of the sacrificial service which alone would enable the Jews once more to abide by all the provisions of the divinely revealed law.

Anything short of that totality of observance would of necessity be regarded as an "exilic" condition. Nor did the absence of animal sacrifices exhaust the religious meaning of "exile." "Exile," as understood by the Jewish mystics, was not only the "exile" of Israel, but also the "exile of the Divine Presence." God Himself, so it was taught, had "gone into exile." The Kingdom of God was incomplete, and would only be perfected when the whole world would acknowledge the Unity and the sovereignty of God. The period before that universal acknowledgment is the pre-messianic period, the period of "exile." It is the period, to use an apt phrase coined by Martin Buber, of the "Eclipse of God."

It is true, the early Reformers did not bewail the absence of Temple and sacrifice, and they did not desire their restoration. If the religious aspect of "exile" had been confined to this, the Reformers could not have been blamed for excluding it from their considerations. But, as we have seen, the religious aspect of "exile," even as understood by traditional Judaism, goes far beyond the confines of the sacrificial cult. Even if the whole sacrificial legislation had been excluded from consideration, it is still true, and it was already true in the nineteenth century, that man does not live up to the fullest of his spiritual potential, that various factors restrain him from abiding by the totality of the divine Law—however he may construe that Law. There is a boastfulness and a *hybris*, which do not correspond to the humility inculcated by religion, in the claim voiced by anyone that he and his generation represent the climax of the millennial messianic hope, that man, by his own efforts, has finally succeeded in establishing the Kingdom of God.

We can understand, and even sympathize with, the men of certain periods in history who were animated by such feelings. But such historical understanding does not imply agreement in objective fact. Who, today, can honestly claim that the Eclipse of God has been lifted, that the messianic era has already dawned, and that man is living up to his fullest spiritual potential? No, if "exile" be conceived as the pre-messianic era, then it must regretfully be admitted that both God and man are still "in exile."

What applies to the human condition in general applies no less to the specific Jewish situation. American Jews cannot claim that, as of this moment, they are realizing their Jewish potential to the fullest, that they are encountering no hindrances along the path of their Jewish self-fulfilment. Economic and social considerations are often responsible for compromises in the realm of religious observance. Christmas is an annual problem in American Jewish life, for American Jews have not yet developed that inner strength and outer dignity which would enable them to let their Christian neighbors observe Christmas—without either fulminating against public Christmas observances, or slavishly imitating Christmas practices in their own homes. Jewish worship services are conducted not only in accordance with the inherent dynamics of Jewish religious development, but also with a constant eye on the lookout for possible non-Jewish reactions. And the whole area of Jewish education still leaves very much to be desired—to give but a few illustrations.

If, therefore, the Israeli and the Zionist describe Jewish life in America in pre-messianic or "exilic" terms, such description cannot be rejected by the American Jew as false. That is, if the Israeli and the Zionist should indeed refer to the religious and spiritual implications of "exile." But if such a description is meant to be *political,* if it is meant to be contrasted with a presumed political superiority of the Israeli Jew over the American Jew, then the American Jew may retort, in gratitude and in pride, that he, of all people, is not aware of any "subjugation to foreign kingdoms." On the political level of "exile," or the absence thereof, there is, to say the very least, parity between the Israeli and the American Jew.

But if, as so often happens, the Israeli should wish to exclude his own country from the category of "exile," in **both its political and its spiritual** connotations, then he must be met with the incredulity born of a deeper understanding of the traditional concepts of "exile" and messianic redemption—in all their religious, political, geographical, and temporal dimensions. The traditional Jewish messianic hope does not permit the concept of redeemed enclaves in an unredeemed world. There can be no messianic fulfilment, in the true sense, for Jews if the rest of the world has experienced no such fulfilment. However national and particularistic some of the elements were which went into the making of the traditional messianic hope, one aspect was never lost sight of: the messianic redemption had to be universal, it had to be the salvation of all mankind. "Nation shall not lift up sword against nation; neither shall they learn war any more." To the extent to which this remains an unfulfilled hope, to that extent no country on earth—the State of Israel included—can claim messianic fulfilment and the end of the period of "exile."

The concept of "exile," rightly understood, is a valuable, an indispensable, category of religious thought, and motivation of religious living. If, therefore, the State of Israel challenges American Jews by invoking the concept of "exile," American Jews ought to be grateful for that challenge. But it is a challenge which the American Jew will have to meet on his own ground, and not by escaping into the dreamworld of building messianically redeemed enclaves elsewhere. Alas, it happens all too often that American Jews are left with the feeling that they have done their duty to Judaism if they have helped to establish Israeli institutions —to the greater or lesser neglect of the institutions of American Judaism. It then becomes very easy for them to turn around, and, in comparison with the concrete reality of Israel, to denigrate the Judaism of their own country. And yet, **the institutions themselves are** but the outward shell of an inner spirit, of a spirit which is no more in evidence in the State of Israel than it is in the United States. If, therefore, there is hope that this spirit may yet be instilled into Israel, there is no less hope that this spirit may likewise come to rest upon the institutions of American Judaism.

The Talmud knows of the "jealousy of the scholars" which leads to the "increase of wisdom." This may not be the kind of challenge with which the State of Israel wants to confront the American Jew. But it is the only kind of challenge which the American Jew can legitimately discern out of the whole welter of Zionist propaganda. And, if the American Jew does indeed take up this particular challenge, then— although not thus intended by the theoreticians of Zionism —the State of Israel will have had its beneficial effect upon the largest Jewry in the Diaspora.

CHAPTER FIVE

"Life Insurance" Against Anti-Semitism?

Jews today may, or may not, engage in metaphysical speculation. What has been said in our previous chapters about the state of religion in Israel and in America may be of interest to some, of utter indifference to others. But there is one subject which holds the interest of all Jews, one topic which is on the agenda of religionist and secularist alike. And that is anti-Semitism. The contemporaries of what happened at Auschwitz and Buchenwald cannot afford to ignore this subject. It will always hold their attention, and any endeavor to fight the resurgence of the phenomenon thus described is assured of their faithful financial support.

German Jews committed the fatal mistake of not taking anti-Semitism seriously enough, at least, not before it was too late. Their insistence that "it cannot happen here!" has made other Jews wary of repeating that phrase—however fortunate and peaceful the circumstances under which they may be living, however remote the possibility of serious manifestations of anti-Semitism in their particular environment. Many, therefore, whose whole outlook on life would preclude the acceptance of a Zionist philosophy nevertheless let Zionism go unchallenged, because—in retrospect—the Zionist diagnosis of anti-Semitism appears to have been correct. How many Jewish lives could have been saved had there but been a Jewish State before the outbreak of World War II? And who knows, the day may come when we may need such a place of refuge again!

Zionism encourages this state of mind. When all other arguments fail, the threat of anti-Semitism will be used to clinch Zionism's case. Historically, moreover, as we have had frequent occasion to note, anti-Semitism is also the starting point of political Zionism. Anti-Semitism, argued Pinsker, is caused by the absence of a Jewish Homeland. Nations respect one another only so long as they can anticipate reciprocity in the extending of hospitality, i.e., as long as they all have a Homeland of their own. The anomaly of the Jews consists in their lack of a Homeland. As a nation without a Homeland, they create a ghostlike impression among their host-peoples. By not having a country of their own, they are completely unlike the other nations. And there is a general fear of ghosts, a universal dislike of the unlike, which, *vis-à-vis* the Jews, manifests itself in the phenomenon of anti-Semitism. Let the Jews acquire a Homeland of their own, and thereby become like all the other nations, and the psychopathic cause of anti-Semitism will be cured.

Herzl's approach to the same subject has already been repeatedly mentioned. It leads to the same conclusion: let the Jews go to their own Homeland, and anti-Semitism will disappear. All other attempts to deal with anti-Semitism are doomed to fail.

Since May 1948, a Jewish State has been in existence. But it does not exist in a vacuum. It is surrounded by a hostile Arab world—hostile, precisely because it does exist. And it has its being within a world torn by the power struggle between East and West. Consequently, the existence of the Jewish State has led to an increase, rather than a decrease, of anti-Jewish feeling in the Muslim world; nor, in view of the support which the State of Israel is receiving from the West, has the precarious position of the Jews in the Soviet orbit been eased. These are circumstances which neither

Pinsker nor Herzl envisaged; and because they did not, and perhaps could not, envisage them, it may not be fair to judge their theories by the yardstick of present-day realities.

By the same token, however, it may also not be fair to continue mouthing the slogans of "classical" political Zionism. Yet that is precisely what Zionists are doing. Emigrate to Israel, they say to the Jews of the Diaspora, for what happened in Germany can happen in other places as well— even in America! Only in the State of Israel is the Jew really safe.

Predictions about anti-Semitism, one way or another, are precarious; but the presentation of the State of Israel as a kind of "life insurance" for the American Jew against anti-Semitism merits a little closer analysis—not in terms of yesterday's Zionist ideology, but in terms of today's realities.

To begin with, let us take the assertion that the Jew is safe only in the State of Israel. If "safety" is understood in any physical sense, then the assertion is a blatant untruth. There may be country clubs in America which do not admit Jews as members, and there may be positions in commerce and in industry which American Jews find difficult to obtain. There may even be anti-Semitic demonstrations and anti-Semitic literature. But the five and a half million American Jews can be reasonably sure that they will not suddenly be shot at. The Jews in the State of Israel can have no such certainty. They are surrounded on three sides by Arab nations sworn to their destruction. (The fourth side is the Mediterranean Sea.) There is hardly a week when there is not some kind of "border incident." There is hardly a month when at least one person does not get shot.

From a certain point of view, it may be more "glorious" to die "in defense of the Jewish Homeland" than to be called a "dirty Jew" on some side street in New York. But we are dealing with an argument based on "safety," and not with an appeal to die gloriously. Not that there is any absence of the latter for domestic consumption in the State of Israel itself. The situation calls for it. Life in Israel breeds the besieged-fortress mentality; and Massadah, where, during the Jewish rebellion against Rome in the first century, the defenders slaughtered one another in preference to being taken captive by the victorious Romans, has become an important national shrine. Israel's soldiers are being sworn in there.

The fact remains that the State of Israel does not excel by the "safety" which it offers. And history has already recorded the destruction of two Jewish states in that particular territory, in 586 B.C.E., and in 70 C.E.

Israel's War of Independence has shown that Israel's army can hold its own against the combined armies of Israel's Arab neighbors. Israel's Sinai exploit, in 1956, has demonstrated Israel's military valor against the Egyptians. But it has demonstrated something else as well. Israel was forced to vacate her conquests, not because of any military weakness, but because the Great Powers had decided that she should do so. For, in 1956, the Great Powers did not think that it was in their own best interest that Israel should occupy Egyptian territory. When the United States joined Russia in the demand for it, Prime Minister Ben-Gurion ordered the retreat.

For, if truth is to be told, the political leaders of Israel understand very well that Israel does not exist in a political vacuum. If Israel did not have the political support of the West, she would disappear tomorrow. If the Arab nations did not know of the West's interest in keeping the peace of the Near East, they would not think twice about utilizing the skill of German scientists and the accumulated armaments from the Eastern Bloc in wiping Israel off the map. It is, in other words, the good will of the West which is helping Israel to maintain her very existence.

We are now asked by Zionist leaders to reckon with the possibility that what happened in Germany may happen in the United States as well, and to draw the only possible

conclusion: Jewish emigration from America to Israel. But
what was it that happened in Germany? The adoption of
anti-Semitism as the official policy of the government, and,
consequently, the promotion of anti-Semitism as a regular
component of the operations of government.

Leaving aside the question whether, in a pluralistic society
like that of the United States, the German kind of govern-
ment-sponsored anti-Semitism would even be possible, we
may, for argument's sake, adopt the dire Zionist prognosis.
Suppose, then, that the government of the United States
adopts anti-Semitism as its official policy. What then? Are
we to assume that an anti-Semitic Washington will continue
to maintain friendly relations with the State of Israel, pro-
moting the latter's welfare both politically and economically?
Will such an anti-Semitic American government make it
its business to keep Arab hostilities in check? The situation
needs only to be spelled out in concrete terms to demon-
strate the ludicrous nature of the Zionist argument.

Jews dedicated to the realization of the American Dream
will continue to believe, to hope, and to pray that "what
happened in Germany" cannot and will not happen in the
United States. If, God forbid, they should turn out to be
wrong, if America should become so untrue to her own
nature that Jewish existence within her borders becomes
precarious, then it is likewise impossible to conceive that
tiny Israel will fare any better. On the contrary, an official
adoption of anti-Semitism by the government of the United
States would represent the "green light" for the Arabs to
go ahead with their plan of "driving the Jews into the sea."

Zionist politicians have all kinds of reasons for wanting to
encourage Jewish immigration from the United States. Israel
needs Western "know-how." Israel has to build up her manpower—for industry, for agriculture, and for her army. Above
all, Israel is looking for immigration from the West in order
to counterbalance her rapidly increasing Oriental population. Such are the real reasons which induce Zionist leaders

to call for immigration from America. And there may very well be some American Jews who are sufficiently in sympathy with Israel's needs to heed the Zionist call. But hiding projects demanded by the political needs of the State of Israel behind an appeal to the Jew's only-too-well-founded fear of anti-Semitism, trying to "sell" Israel to the American Jew as a kind of "life insurance," amounts to a cynical espousal of the doctrine that the end hallows the means, a doctrine which is not any less objectionable just because, in this instance, the beneficiaries, as well as the victims, happen to be Jews.

In fairness to Zionist political leadership it must be stated that not all Zionist leaders continue to use the threat of anti-Semitism as a compelling argument to convince the Jews of America. Some, like Mr. Ben-Gurion, use the very decline of anti-Semitism in the United States as the basis of their appeal. They admit that American Jews are in no physical danger. But, just because of that, American Jews are said to be in danger of "being loved to death." That danger is said to consist of the ease with which Jews are able to assimilate. Statistics on intermarriage are used to prove that, in the absence of anti-Semitism, the Jewish group is gradually bound to disappear. Consequently, only immigration to the State of Israel can enable the American Jew to survive.

The latter argument is, of course, based on a certain value judgment placed upon the term "assimilation," and it will be our task in Chapter Six to subject both the term and the value judgment to some closer scrutiny. For our present purposes it is sufficient to know that Zionists use two mutually exclusive arguments to achieve the same result. It is either a case of "what happened in Germany" being bound to happen in America—the American Jew, therefore, had better run for safety to the State of Israel. Or it is a case of "what happened in Germany" *not* happening in America. Therefore, let him beware of the *danger* of the *absence* of anti-Semitism, and let him betimes seek refuge in the State of Israel.

The fact that both arguments are being used may serve as additional proof for our previous assumption that the *raison d'état* of the State of Israel, rather than concern for the safety or otherwise of the Jews of America, determines the appeal for American Jewish immigration. Under the circumstances, the "life insurance" theory should at last be given its well-deserved burial.

CHAPTER SIX

Once More "The Mission of Israel"

There is much misunderstanding between the Jews of the State of Israel and the Jews living elsewhere. There is misunderstanding about the demands which the former may legitimately make upon the latter. There is misunderstanding about the expectations which the latter may rightly have of the former. Such misunderstanding is in no small measure due to the fact that there is considerable unclarity about the meaning of the entity called "Jewish People." There is great difficulty in defining the "Jew." We noted in Chapter One that the question, "Who is a Jew?" has consistently eluded an adequate answer in the State of Israel. We cannot blame the State of Israel for failing to provide such an answer. Others have not found it either.

The answer, obviously, cannot be found in the realm of racial theories. People of all races and colors can seek admission to Judaism; and, over the course of the millennia, many have done so. Among Jews today all racial types are represented, so that the factor which makes them "Jews" cannot be one of race.

But the Jews are also not a nation, in the sense in which there are nations like the French, the British, and the Italian. There is no such thing as a common Jewish territory, a government to which allegiance is owed by all Jews, or even an everyday language which is common to all Jews. There undoubtedly was such a thing as a Jewish nation in historical antiquity. But that came to an end some twenty centuries ago. And there is the endeavor to create the Jewish nation anew in our time. The State of Israel is engaged in this task. But it has jurisdiction only over its own citizens. Besides, the nation which is coming into being in the State of Israel is an "Israeli," rather than a "Jewish," nation, for Israeli citizenship is by no means restricted to Jews. There are Christian Israelis, and there are Muslim Israelis. It is precisely in defining the "Jewish" aspect of its nationhood that the government of the State of Israel has repeatedly landed itself in a welter of confusion and dilemmas.

To assume the existence of a Jewish nation just because the Israelis are trying to create one is a severe case of question-begging. Even if Israeli citizenship were available to Jews only, the most that could be said about it then would be that *some* Jews, i.e., those living in the State of Israel, constitute a "Jewish nation." But since the Jewish inhabitants of the State of Israel represent but a fraction of world Jewry, nothing would be gained thereby in terms of defining the nature of Jews as a whole.

The problem is compounded still further once it is realized that the Jews do not even constitute a religion, if religion be understood on the analogy of the ecclesiastical framework of Protestantism and Catholicism. A Protestant who ceases to believe in Protestant dogmas, and who does not practice the religion in which he was reared, also ceases to be a Protestant. The same applies to the Catholic. But it does not apply to the Jew.

There is no supreme Jewish ecclesiastical authority which could read a Jew out of the faith. And even if such an authority were in existence, the very documents of religious law, which it would have to administer, preclude the possibility of "leaving Judaism." According to traditional Jewish law, a Jew who converts to another faith continues to be a Jew—a bad Jew, or a sinful Jew, but still a Jew. The Covenant which God made with the fathers does not allow for

the possibility of "opting out." When, recently, the Supreme
Court of the State of Israel had to rule on the eligibility
of the Jewish convert to Catholicism, Brother Daniel, to
obtain Israeli citizenship under Israel's "Law of Return," it
denied his eligibility on the grounds of the current understanding of this *secular* law. But it admitted that, according
to Jewish *religious* law, the monk was still a Jew.

We are, at this moment, concerned with the definition
which Judaism gives of itself in its own authoritative sources.
One might argue, of course, that, ideally, a man ought to
be given the right to determine his own affiliation, a right
which, in the case of Brother Daniel, would entitle him to
be considered a Jew, and which, in the case of others born
of Jewish parents, would respect their desire not to be known
as Jews. But we have to meet the facts as we find them,
and leave our suggestions for improvements, if any, for
another occasion. And the facts as we find them leave us in
no doubt that Judaism does not allow for the possibility of
"opting out," that the Jewish frame of reference is, therefore, broader than that of the ecclesiastical organization
exemplified by both Protestantism and Catholicism. If the
latter two are taken as a yardstick, then Judaism is not a
"religion." For that matter, even in those circles which
insist most emphatically that Judaism is a religion (rather
than a race, or a nation), little attention, if any, is paid to
the criteria by which one's qualifications of belonging to
that religion are to be measured. There has been no attempt
to read the completely nonobservant and the completely
nonbelieving "out of the faith."

No, the categories of race, nation, and religion are utterly
useless when it comes to defining the Jew. In desperation,
some have suggested that the Jews are a "cultural" group.
In the light of what has been said about "Jewish culture"
in our previous chapters, it ought to be obvious that this
definition is no more felicitous than the other three. It is
one of the most urgent problems of the State of Israel to

create a uniform culture for its inhabitants, because such a
culture is not yet in existence; and the various cultures which
Jews have brought with them to the State of Israel tend to
divide, rather than unite, the populace.

Perhaps the Jews simply elude the attempt at defining
them. Perhaps there is no ready-made definition which could
do justice to the phenomenon. The Biblical writers seem to
have had an inkling of this. They apply the same Hebrew
word, *ehad* ("unique"), to the God of Israel as well as to
the People of Israel. (See Deuteronomy 6:4, and I Chronicles 17:21; and cf. the Babylonian Talmud, *Berakhoth* 6a.)
Just as the God of Israel defies classification among the gods
of pagan antiquity, so is Israel a people which "shall not be
reckoned among the nations." (Numbers 23:9.)

It is one thing to speak, in the abstract, of a unique phenomenon defying definition. It is another thing, again, to
have to deal with concrete reality. The Talmud could not
avoid laying down some ground rules, and setting up some
criteria as to who is to be considered a Jew. According to
the formulation of the Talmud, a Jew is either a person
born of a Jewish mother, or a person of non-Jewish antecedents who has undergone the Jewish rites of conversion.

Stripped of its legalistic terminology, what the formulation
of the Talmud amounts to is the assertion that Judaism is a
"family matter." A Jew is a member of the family of Abraham, the first Jew. Like all other families, this particular
family reckons its membership in terms of those who were
born into it, and in terms of those who came into it from
other families. Like all other families, this particular family
also has its "black sheep," its "skeletons in the closet," and
those of its members who prefer not to be known as belonging to this family.

But, unlike other families, this particular family knows
itself to be standing in a unique relationship to the Sovereign
of the Universe, a relationship which has been the decisive

influence on the formation of the family tradition, to such
an extent that, for some four thousand years, the family has
seen its very reason for existence in the mission of bringing
other families into the same kind of relationship with God.
"In thee shall all the families of the earth be blessed."
(Genesis 12:3.) To the accident of birth, therefore, Abraham's family added the awareness of a covenant relationship
with God as the determining feature of family "belonging-
ness." And from that awareness there flowed the sense of
noblesse oblige. This latter might be expressed by the
Biblical phrase, "a kingdom of priests and a holy nation."
It might be paraphrased by such Biblical images as those
of "the servant of the Lord," or "a light unto the nations."
It might inspire a Judah Halevi to think of Israel as "the
heart of the nations." And it might lead the Jewish theologians of the nineteenth century to include "the Mission
of Israel" in their formulations of the essence of Judaism.
But whatever the metaphor, the image, or the formulation,
what all of them have in common is the sense of *noblesse
oblige,* of destiny and of purpose, without which the family
would have seen no reason to maintain itself when prudence
and mere self-interest would have cautioned against the
stubborn loyalty to the family tradition.

Such being the case, it is not surprising that historical
exigencies and purposeful choice have combined to invest
the members of this family with a remarkable adaptability
to the mere accidents of mundane existence. Members of
this family, as seminomads, have tended their flocks in the
oases of the Negev. Members of this family have been slaves
in Egypt. Members of this family have lived in Palestine
under various forms of political organization—the tribe,
the tribal federation, the monarchy, the theocracy, the
colonial territory of a foreign power. Members of this
family have lived as Judaean exiles in Babylonia—some of
them availing themselves of the opportunity to return to the

land of their fathers, when this opportunity was afforded them, and others, the majority, preferring to stay on in Babylonia.

Some members of this family have lived, and died, as fanatical patriots of the ancestral soil. Others have voluntarily left it, while Temple and State were still in existence, to seek their fortunes elsewhere—glorying in Roman citizenship, and building synagogues throughout the Mediterranean world. Members of this family, while enriching the family's spiritual and philosophical heritage, have acted as high government officials in Muslim Spain; others, in less fortunate circumstances, suffered persecution in the lands of medieval Christendom.

In general, whenever the environment permitted it, members of this family took an active part in the environment's culture and civilization, without feeling in the least that their family tradition would thereby be compromised. Yet, by the same token, whenever members of this family were excluded from the cultural and social life of the countries of their abode, they tended to become ingrown and withdrawn, dreaming, instead, about a messianic return to their ancestors' old Homeland.

But, throughout the family's long history, loyalty to the family tradition was never measured in terms of the language which members of this family spoke, or of the culture in which they participated. Not even in matters of religion was absolute uniformity ever a desired goal. Palestine in the Rabbinic period knew of variations in religious practice between the inhabitants of Galilee and the inhabitants of Judaea, not to mention the even wider differences between Jewish religious practice in Palestine and that of Babylonia. Later on, Sepharadim and Ashkenazim, Jews of Spanish and Portuguese provenance, on the one hand, and Jews of German and Polish origin, on the other, mutually respected each other's variant liturgical traditions, and still do. Basic and fundamental to them all, though, was faith in the One God to Whose worship the family had ever been dedicated. This, and the desire to ápply the dictates of the Torah to the constantly changing conditions of life, as well as the hope that, "in the end of days," all mankind would join in these pursuits, thereby justifying the hopes and the aspirations, the prayers and the martyrdom, the sufferings and the perseverance, which have been the family's millennial heritage.

There have been members of the family who have severed their ties, just as there have been members of other families who, in the course of history, have joined the family of Abraham. The newcomers were attracted by this family's particular tradition and vocation. And some of them have turned out to be the most active and loyal members.

Moreover, the family tradition has always been broad enough to give scope to the most varied temperaments and inclinations. Of course, there have been occasional family squabbles and bickerings. Rationalists have been at odds with mystics, prophets with priests, traditionalists with reformers, and universalists with particularists. Yet it is part of the genius of this family that time is quickly able to let acrimonies die down, and to create the broader vision in which apparent irreconcilables are reconciled. There is enough of a recognition, among members of this family, of the greatness of God, and enough of a healthy awareness of human limitations, to permit the frequent application of the incomparable Talmudic wisdom which proclaimed, "Both points of view are the words of the Living God."

The family has been immeasurably enriched by the various cultures and civilizations to which its members have been exposed, and in which they have taken part. The culture of the Canaanites, the original inhabitants of Palestine, the civilization of Babylonia, the family's first home environment, the achievements of Hellas and of Rome, the thinking of the medieval schoolmen, both Christian and

Muslim, the challenge of the Enlightenment, of German Idealism, of American Pragmatism, of European Existentialism, have all, in one way or another, forced a restatement, in contemporary terms, of the family tradition. They have all contributed, in some measure or other, to the deepening of the family heritage, and to the potential of its survival through the generations.

It is at this point that a word should be said about "assimilation." We have seen in Chapter Five that "assimilation" is a bad word in the Zionist vocabulary. "Assimilation" is a danger; "assimilation" is a threat. It is the fear of "assimilation" which should drive the Jews of America to seek refuge in the State of Israel—if the other fear, that of anti-Semitism, can no longer be relied upon to do so.

But what is assimilation? Actually, as has long been known, there is both an active and a passive kind of assimilation. If the lion eats the lamb, then the lamb, nourishing the lion's flesh and bones, and ceasing to exist as a separate "lambish" entity, becomes "assimilated" to the lion. This is the passive kind of assimilation. However, the lion, in devouring the lamb, is also engaged in a process of assimilation. He is "assimilating" the nutritional substance of the lamb to his own "lionish" organism. In fact, he is doing so precisely the better to maintain his own "lionhood." This would be the active variety of assimilation. It is clear that the only "bad" kind of assimilation—if value judgments are called for at all—is the passive variety. As for the active kind, there simply is no life on earth without it. Not only is this true in realms biological. The same applies, with equal force, to cultural and spiritual life.

When ancient Israel turned from nomadic pursuits to the settled life of agriculture in Canaan, it did not shrink from "assimilating" the agricultural festivals of the Canaanite calendar. It assimilated them actively by making them serve its own religious needs; and Judaism is the richer for having

Passover, Pentecost, and Tabernacles. But when Israel also began to exchange its God for the *baalim* of Canaan, it was in grave danger of being itself passively assimilated; and only the work of the Hebrew Prophets saved Israel from such a fate.

The literature of Rabbinic Judaism—the Mishnah, the Midrash, and the Talmud—is full of traces of a very active assimilation. Not only is the language of Rabbinic literature shot through with linguistic borrowings from Latin, Greek, and Persian, but its very legal concepts and the organization of its materials are heavily indebted to the legal systems of the non-Jewish environment. Yet this pronounced "assimilation" insured the very survival of Judaism, not its demise. For the process of assimilation was undertaken to maintain and to safeguard the family tradition within an environment and a state of societal evolution which differed markedly from the simple agricultural life which is reflected in Biblical literature.

So far we have dealt with relatively simple illustrations of the phenomenon, and the instances described are safely connected with the very distant past. The matter becomes more complicated once we look at illustrations closer to home.

When the East European Jew, in the nineteenth century, looked at his fellow Jews west of the Oder and Elbe rivers, he was shocked and dismayed at the German Jews' "assimilation." They were speaking German, while he communicated in Yiddish. They dressed in central European style, while he donned his gaberdine and *streimel*. They sent their sons and daughters to the universities, while he sent his sons to the *yeshivah*. They conducted their religious services according to the canons of Western decorum, while he was attached to the informality of his own unpretentious conventicle. They socialized with their non-Jewish neighbors, while he sought his contacts exclusively among his own Jewish circles. There could be no doubt, as far as the East European Jew was concerned, that the German Jew was bound to disappear.

The fact of the matter is that the German Jews were indeed "assimilating." But, while the East European Jew saw this assimilation as being of the passive kind, the German Jew was, in fact, assimilating actively. He assimilated those aspects of Western culture which helped him maintain his Judaism within that particular environment. This is not to say that there were not among German Jews, as there are among all Jewish groups, those who preferred to sever their family ties, those, that is to say, who assimilated passively. They did so via the baptismal font, but not by means of decorous *Jewish* worship services, not by means of the pursuit and support of the scientific study of Judaism, and not through the creation and espousal of such "assimilated" systems of Jewish philosophy and theology as are associated with the names of Hermann Cohen, Leo Baeck, and Franz Rosenzweig.

Moreover, the East European Jew was hardly aware of the extent of his own assimilation. The language he spoke was the German of an earlier century, mixed with Hebraic and Slavonic elements—a language utterly incomprehensible to any Sepharadi or Oriental Jew, and in itself clear evidence of an earlier stage of "assimilation." The garb he wore was the garb of the Poles of an earlier generation. The "Jewish music" he sang in his synagogues was the music of his Slavonic environment; and even the teachings of his Hasidic mentors bore the traces of elements at home within the Russian Orthodox form of Christian mysticism.

Again, when the modern Israeli Jew looks across the ocean at the American Jew, he finds the latter speaking English, while he is speaking Hebrew. The American Jew is thoroughly at home within his American environment, while the Israeli feels at home in Israel. Whereas the Israeli Jew has few contacts with non-Jews, the American Jew is increasingly establishing such contacts. At a time when the Israeli Jew is engaged in the creation of a distinctively Israeli culture, the American Jew actively participates in the creation of American culture. While the Israeli Jew is hemmed in by enemies around his borders, the American Jew has developed an outlook in consonance with the vast expanses of his own free homeland. And the Israeli Jew is convinced that the American Jew is involved in a process of passive assimilation, which must inevitably lead to his disappearance.

It is, no doubt, true that there are Jews in America who may be on their "way out." There have always been such Jews, in all ages and climes. The independent and sovereign Northern Kingdom of Israel, in the Biblical period, was on its "way out," not only because of the superior forces of its enemies, but also because its own citizens had become passively assimilated to the dominant pagan culture of the time. And, during the Second Jewish Commonwealth in Judaea, there was a whole party of Jews, the so-called Hellenists, who were ready to exchange their Jewish loyalties for those of Hellenism; and only the valor of the Hasmoneans prevented the whole people from going the same way. It would be foolish to deny that life in a free society, such as that of the United States, facilitates the "exit" of those Jews whose ties to Judaism have become tenuous, just as it increases the challenge to those who, of their own free volition, have opted to remain faithful. This is both the price for, and the advantage of, life under freedom. But the Jews who have chosen the "way out" do not tread it by actively creating the institutions which will most efficiently keep alive the family tradition of the family of Abraham within the American setting. Yet most American Jews are doing just that; and the State of Israel is not a little indebted to that devotion of the Jews of America.

What the Israeli Jew does not see, or does not care to
see, is that the American Jew is enjoying an unprecedented
opportunity for growth and development, and that in a
country where he is granted recognition as one of the
three major religious groups—a recognition quite out of
proportion to the actual population statistics. What he does
not see is how the free democratic spirit of America has
taught Jews of all different shades of religious opinion, not
only to live peacefully together in mutual recognition of
each other's right to exist, but also to cooperate in projects
of common interest.

And what the Israeli Jew also does not see is the degree
of his own "assimilation." The mere attempt to capture the
essence of Jewish being within the categories of nineteenth-
century European nationalism is as blatant a case of assimilation as any with which the American Jew could be charged.
The Hebrew language he speaks, though written in a Semitic
alphabet and using an—although decreasing—amount of
Classical Hebrew grammar, is syntactically more and more
approaching the pattern of modern European languages.
It is not the language of the Bible; and Rabbinic texts are
almost as difficult to master for the Israeli Jew as they are
for his non-Israeli cousin in the Diaspora. It was perhaps
just a trifle more serious than a mere joke when some of
the older immigrants from Eastern Europe called the Israel-
born generation of Jews, "Hebrew-speaking Gentiles."

If "assimilation" is something positive, then the Israeli
variety of it is no more blameworthy than the "assimilation"
of Jews in any other environment. If, however, it is something negative, as the Zionists tend to make us believe, then
the Israeli Jew is in no position whatsoever to cast aspersions
on anyone else.

The "threat of assimilation," therefore, turns out to be
but another propaganda slogan. The fact that it is being
used, however, points up a real and fundamental problem
which must be faced. The Israeli, dependent as he is upon

the support of Jews from abroad, is becoming aware of an ever widening gulf between himself and the Jews elsewhere. There is no common language, no common culture, no common literature—at least, there is not once the reality behind the propaganda claims is honestly examined.

This in itself need not spell the alienation of Israeli Jewry from the rest of the members of Abraham's family. After all, the Jews of England, France, Germany, Italy, and America have also not shared a common language, culture, or literature. Still, they did not feel alienated from one another. They had common religious ties, and the philanthropic bonds that grew out of them. International religious organizations, like the *Agudath Israel,* the World Union for Progressive Judaism, and the World Council of Synagogues, philanthropic organizations like the *Hilfsverein,* the *Alliance Israélite Universelle,* or the Joint Distribution Committee, all helped to bridge the distances between various culture and language groups. When all was said and done, the family tradition of the family of Abraham was strongly felt and fostered wherever Jews lived.

But it is precisely this family tradition which has fallen on evil days in the State of Israel. To the extent to which it is manifest there, in its medieval Orthodox formulation, it is liable to repel rather than to attract and bind together. Even worse, where it is not manifest, its absence is proclaimed so proudly and so belligerently that the cutting of the religious tie is made to look like a glorious achievement, rather than as the grievous loss which it is.

If, then, the Jews in Israel are no longer bound to their fellow-Jews in other lands by that which, for millennia, has bound Jews together, there are but two options for the Israeli. He can cut himself loose from his Jewish moorings, and there are Israelis who try to do just that, who prefer to be known as Israelis or as Hebrews, rather than as Jews —not to mention the fringe-group of the "Canaanites." Or he can try to impose his own yardsticks and definitions upon

the Jews of the Diaspora. The latter is the way chosen by
the Zionist propaganda effort. Not that the Israeli Jews
should find their way to the religious tradition; but the
Diaspora Jew must adopt the philosophy of Jewish nationalism. Not that the Israeli Jews constitute one branch, out
of many, of Abraham's family; but whoever wants to maintain his good standing within the family must settle in
Israel. Not that Judaism implies spiritual, cultural, and
social endeavor wherever the Jew may live; but the "full
Jewish life" is restricted to the confines of the State of
Israel.

It is unlikely that, on such a basis, the Jews of Israel will
for very long maintain their connection with the rest of
Jewry. Judaism has existed for millennia without benefit of
an Israeli State, and, conceivably, it could do so again.
And yet, it would be an unspeakable pity if all the sacrifice
of lives, of effort, of energy, and of wealth, which has gone
into the making of the State of Israel were to have been
wasted on the creation of yet another temporary concentration of Jews going the way of other such concentrations
which, from time to time in Jewish history, have lost their
touch with the main body of Judaism, and have atrophied.
The possibility does indeed exist. But so does another.
And that other possibility is connected with the very doctrine
which Zionists have always ridiculed and attacked: the
doctrine of the "Mission of Israel."

The "Mission of Israel," as understood by the great
Jewish thinkers of the nineteenth century, does not posit
the formation of a Jewish nation and the creation of a Jewish
State. As God's "kingdom of priests and holy people," the
Jews are to work for the establishment of God's Kingdom
on Earth throughout their habitations. But the "Mission of
Israel" also does not intrinsically rule out the possibility
that *some* Jews might make their contribution to this
"Mission" by leading a corporate national existence, although,
admittedly, it is a possibility which was not anticipated by

the theologians of the nineteenth century. Members of the
family of Abraham have been called upon to witness to their
faith in all sorts of conditions and under all kinds of circumstances. It may well be that some of them, in our own day,
have been called upon to witness through their own state.
The witness of the Jew in America will be different from the
witness of the Jew in the State of Israel. But who is to say
which form of the testimony is more vital to the divine
economy? Both of them may be equally needed.

The Jew of the Diaspora makes his contribution through
the constant give-and-take in the continuous confrontation
of his ancestral tradition with the spiritual and intellectual
currents and crosscurrents of his environment. This demands a unique combination of loyalty and open-minded-
ness, of tradition and adaptability. It makes him a full
member of society, and an active participant in its culture.
Yet it also provides him with a yardstick with which to
measure the achievements of society, a set of values by
which and through which he can always transcend the
status quo. And from the attachment to such values there
flows the Jew's desire to share them with others, to make
them part of his country and his nation. The demands of
justice tempered by mercy, the sanctity of the home, the
striving for peace, the honesty in business dealings, the
importance of intellectual pursuits, the support of the under-
privileged, the recognition that all of man's deeds are under
the judgment of God—those are some of the values to the
realization of which in society the "Mission of Israel" obli-
gates the Jew of the Diaspora.

Often his concern is shared by others, and his task is
thereby made a little easier. Sometimes he finds himself
without many other supporters. But, in either case, he makes
his contribution, or tries to make it, as a Jewish citizen
of a country made up of citizens belonging to many religious
denominations. Thus, his success or his failure, while bringing him glory or shame, will never be deemed to be the

responsibility of Judaism alone. Judaism makes its contribution, or fails to make it. But the commitments of others
are involved as well.

In the State of Israel, on the other hand, the situation is
quite different. Its role might well be conceived of as Judaism's "showcase" to the world at large, as the testing ground
of Israel's Prophetic faith in action, with Jews as the sole
bearers of responsibility, and Judaism itself as the recipient
of any praise or blame. How seriously do Israelis take the
Biblical view of the "conditional" nature of Jewish occupancy of the soil of the Promised Land? How do they,
actively, manifest their striving for peace? What the State
of Israel does with its minorities, how it conducts itself
in international politics, how it solves its domestic problems, how it lives with its neighbors—all of this will influence
what the world thinks of Judaism as a whole. All of this can
either advance or retard the "Mission of Israel" and the
establishment of God's Kingdom on Earth. If the Jews of
the Diaspora could see the State of Israel in this light, and
if the Israelis themselves could learn to look upon their
state from this perspective, then it will be the "Mission of
Israel," and it alone, which will provide the State of Israel's
much needed bond with the rest of Abraham's family.

That the State of Israel is not yet fulfilling this function
completely is a cause for regret, but not for surprise.
Countries, like individuals, have their growing pains. That,
one day, it may completely live up to these expectations is
our fervent hope and prayer. After all, not every other member of God's "holy people" is at this moment actively engaged
in the "Mission of Israel" either. That, one day, they will
be so engaged is part of the commandment which comes
with the *noblesse oblige* of belonging to the family of Abraham, of being a Jew.

Only the renewed dedication to this family tradition—a
tradition which, as we have seen, transcends all national
and cultural definitions—both in the Diaspora and in the

State of Israel will bring us closer to God's Kingdom. And only the mutual recognition by members of Abraham's family of their respective rights to live and to labor where they choose to do so, and to flourish and to succeed where they desire, will integrate the State of Israel into the millennial pattern of our family tradition.

Glossary

AGUDATH ISRAEL (lit. "Union of Israel"). Originally a world organization of Orthodox Jews, founded in Kattowitz, in 1912. Now also a clericalist political party in the State of Israel.

ALIYAH (lit. "going up"). Following the Biblical use of the verb *'alah* ("to go up") in connection with the entry into Canaan, the noun designates immigration into the Land of Israel.

BETH DIN (lit. "house of judgment"). The local Rabbinical Court. In the State of Israel it is empowered by the government to deal with all matters affecting the personal status of Jews. As of now, membership in these courts is confined to strictly Orthodox rabbis.

DIASPORA (Greek for "dispersion"). The word is used frequently in the Septuagint, the Greek translation of the Bible, to translate Hebrew words denoting both "dispersion" and "exile." It was used to describe the many Jewish communities outside Palestine while the Second Jewish Commonwealth was still in existence, i.e., communities established by *voluntary* emigrants from Palestine. The same word came to be applied to the scattered Jewish communities *after* the destruction of the Second Jewish Commonwealth. In modern times, it has become a matter of ideological debate between Zionists and non-Zionists whether the term Diaspora, as applied to the Jews in America, still has overtones of "exile," or whether it is simply to be taken in its descriptive sense of "dispersion," i.e., the vast geographical spread of Jewish communities.

HAGGADAH (lit. "narration"). Specifically used to describe the liturgical manual for the Passover Eve domestic ceremony. It includes prayers, Biblical and Rabbinic narratives, hymns and songs, commemorating the Exodus from Egypt, and looking forward to the messianic Redemption.

HALAKHAH (lit. "going," "way"). Technical term for the body of Rabbinic Law as a whole, and for the particular construction of a legal provision which, by majority vote, has been accepted as legally binding.

HASHOMER HATZA'IR (lit. "The Young Watchman"). A Zionist-Socialist movement with Marxist leanings. Originally a Jewish Scout movement in Eastern Europe (with branches in other parts of the world, some of them still existing), it became a pioneer movement in Palestine, with its own agricultural settlements. In today's Israel, HASHOMER HATZA'IR is part of the *Mapam* Party, on which see below.

HASIDIM (lit. "the pious ones"). Though most often used in modern writings as the name of the pietistic movement which arose among East European Jews in the eighteenth century, the name had been adopted by earlier groups of pietists throughout the course of Jewish history as well. The first such group arose during the second century B.C.E., and participated, up to a point, in the Maccabean struggle.

HERUTH (lit. "freedom"). Name of the extreme right-wing political party in the State of Israel. It is the successor of the Zionist-Revisionists, and includes members of the terrorist groups of the days of the British Mandate.

HISTADRUTH (lit. "organization"). Abbreviated name of the General Federation of Jewish Workers in the Land of

Israel, the over-all organization of Israel's labor unions.

MAPAI (abbreviation of MIFLEGETH PO'ALE ERETZ ISRAEL, lit.
"Party of the Workers of the Land of Israel"). Israel's
Labor Party.

MAPAM (abbreviation of MIFLEGETH PO'ALIM MEUHEDETH,
lit. "United Workers' Party"). Israel's left-wing (Marxist) Socialist Party.

MIZRACHI (abbreviation of MERKAZ RUCHANI, lit. "spiritual
center"). Originally an organization of Orthodox Zionists, founded in Vilna, in 1902. It was dedicated to
the aim of establishing a Jewish State based on the laws
of the Torah. It became, with the creation of the State
of Israel, one of that country's clericalist political parties.

NATORE KARTHA (lit. "Guardians of the City"). Name adopted
by a group of extremist Orthodox Jews, mostly resident
in Jerusalem's Meah She'arim quarter, who, out of
religious conviction, refuse to recognize the State of
Israel, and who, in their neighborhood, insist—on
occasion, with violence—upon the strictest observance
of Sabbath regulations and on extreme modesty in
feminine dress.

PAKID (lit. "official"). Any kind of official in institutions,
particularly government departments. We have used
the word in the sense of "lower echelon" official. A
senior official would be called a PAKID BAKHIR.

PO'ALE AGUDATH ISRAEL (lit. "The Workers of Agudath
Israel"). The Labor wing of the *Agudath Israel* (see
above), which has its own agricultural settlements.

SANHEDRIN (from the Greek SYNEDRION). The council of
seventy-one elders which was the supreme religious and
legal authority of the Jews in the days of the Second
Jewish Commonwealth.

SHOFAR (lit. "horn"). The ram's horn which is sounded in
the synagogue as part of the New Year observance.
According to ancient Jewish belief, the *shofar* will also
be sounded to herald Messiah's coming.

STREIMEL. Yiddish word for the round hat covered with sable furs, worn by the ultra-Orthodox Jews in Eastern Europe and in Israel.

YESHIVAH, pl. YESHIVOTH (lit. "sitting"). Name of the Talmudic academy already in Rabbinic times. Still used to designate Orthodox institutions of higher Jewish learning in which the curriculum is almost exclusively confined to the study of the Talmud and the Rabbinic codes. (The name has also been adopted by Orthodox Jewish day schools in the United States, in spite of their quite different function.)

Suggestions For Further Reading

The following articles by this author may be of interest to the reader who would like to follow up, in greater detail, some of the subjects touched upon in this book:

"Diaspora Judaism—An Abnormality? The Testimony of History," in *Judaism*, Vol. IX, No. 1 (Winter 1960), pp. 17-28.

"A Fence with Loopholes," in *The Menorah Journal*, Valedictory Issue, 1962, pp. 77-88.

"Ivrith and Leshon Hakodesh," in *The Jewish Spectator*, November, 1958, pp. 8-10.

"The Limits of 'People-Centered' Judaism," in *Commentary*, May, 1959, pp. 387-394.

"The Ninth of Ab Today," in *The Jewish Chronicle*, London, July 29, 1960, p. 15.

"The Problem of 'Recognizing' the Reform Rabbi in the State of Israel," in *Central Conference of American Rabbis Journal*, January, 1965, pp. 4-11.

Review of *Israel: Its Role in Civilization*, ed. Moshe Davis, in *American Jewish Archives*, Vol. IX, No. 2 (October, 1957), pp. 144-148.

"Some Thoughts on Reform Judaism in the State of Israel," in *Central Conference of American Rabbis Journal*, October, 1964, pp. 10-17.

"Tish'ah B'Av in Jerusalem," in *The Jewish Spectator*, June, 1963, pp. 15-18.

"Towards a Definition of our Relation to Israel," in *Central Conference of American Rabbis Journal*, October, 1961, pp. 7-11.

"Who is a Jew?," in *Jewish Frontier*, June, 1959, pp. 6-10.

"Zionism and Reform (Twins of the Nineteenth Century)," in *Jewish Frontier*, March, 1962, pp. 52-57.

Index

Achad Ha'Am, 51, 52
Achduth Avodah, 46
Adler, Felix, 96
Agudath Israel, 44f., 129
Alliance Israélite Universelle, 129
"Altneuland," 24
American Council for Judaism,
    14, 18
American Jewish Committee, 94
Anti-Semitism, 23, 29, 52, 53,
    110f.
Arabs, 52, 53, 55f., 112
Ashkenazim, 25f., 122
Assimilation, 34, 51, 115, 124ff.

Babylonian Exile, 8, 16, 83, 101
Baeck, Leo, 126
Balfour Declaration, 53
Ben-Gurion, David, 28, 59, 61,
    113, 115
Bialik, H. N., 33
B'nai B'rith, 94
British Mandate (of Palestine),
    42, 55
Buber, Martin, 52, 106

Caro, Joseph, 73
Carrigal, Hayyim Isaac, 49
Central Conference of American
    Rabbis, 94
Chief Rabbinate (in Israel), 74
Christmas, 107
Clericalism, 23, 37ff., 40
Cohen, Hermann, 126
Conservative Judaism, 9, 17f., 43,
    71, 75, 97f.

Covenant, 81, 97
Culture, 30ff., 51, 68, 92
Cyrus, 16, 82, 101

Deutero-Isaiah, 8
Diaspora, 102, and *passim.*
Dreyfus *Affaire*, 21

Ecclesiasticus, 102
Emancipation, 8, 15, 19, 86
Eshkol, Levi, 91
Exile, 19, 59, 85, 100ff., and
    passim
Ezekiel, 8

Freud, Sigmund, 32

Ginzburg, Asher, *see* Achad
    Ha'Am
Goldstein, Israel, 89

Hadassah, 60f., 90
Hadoar, 70
Halakhah, 96
Hanukkah, 40, 80
Hashomer Hatza'ir, 61
Hasidim, 64
Hasmoneans, 64, 102, 127
Hebrew, 28, 32f., 51, 68ff., 76,
    128
Heine, Heinrich, 32
Hellenization, 64, 127
Herder, J. G., 32

141

Heruth, 46
Herzl, Theodor, 17, 21, 23f., 27, 51, 52, 111
Hilfsverein, 129
Hillel, 16
Histadruth, 42
Homer, 33

Jerusalem, 34f.
Jesus, 16
"Jewish Consciousness," 39
The Jewish State (by Th. Herzl), 21, 23f.
Jewish Welfare Funds, 94
Joint Distribution Committee, 129
Judah bar Ezekiel, R., 75
Judah Halevi, 50, 83, 121
Judah Maccabee, 64

Kant, Immanuel, 33

Labor Zionist Organization of America, 61
Liberal Party (in Israel), 64

Magnes, Judah L., 52
Maimon, Rabbi J. L., 45, 71ff.
Maimonides, Moses, 73, 75, 84, 104, 105
Mapai, 27, 42, 43, 46, 61
Mapam, 42, 46, 61
Marx, Karl, 32, 42
Massadah, 113
Milhaud, Darius, 31
Mission of Israel, 130ff.
Mizrachi, 42f., 45, 61
Modern Orthodoxy, 9, 75, 95

Natoré Kartha, 14, 18, 44
Nordau, Max, 51

Orthodox Judaism, 14, 21f., 36, 40, 41, 42, 44f., 53, 71ff., 94f.

Passover, 41, 79
Paul, 49
Pentecost, 79
Peoplehood, 18
Pinsker, Leon, 51, 52, 111
"Pittsburgh Platform," 14
Plato, 33
Po'alé Agudath Israel, 44
Psalms of Solomon, 102
Purim, 80

Rabbinic Judaism, 8, 75, 82ff.
Rashi, 75
Ratosh, Jonathan, 71
Reconstructionism, 98
Reform Judaism, 9, 43, 71, 75, 85f., 96f., 104ff.
Rejwan, Nissim, 58
Religion (in the State of Israel), 36ff., and *passim*
Responsa, 76
Resurrection, 41
Rosenblatt, Yossele, 31
Rosenzweig, Franz, 126

Saadia Gaon, 19
Sabbatai Zevi, 16
Sabbath, 37, 79
Sacrifices, 106
Samuel (Babylonian Amora), 104
Sanhedrin, 45, 71ff.
Schechter, Solomon, 18
Secularization, 20f.
Sepharadim, 25f., 122
Shragai, S. Z., 58
Spiritual Center, 67ff.
Stiles, Ezra, 49

Tabernacles, 79
Theocracy, 22

Union of American Hebrew Congregations, 94

United Jewish Appeal, 60, 61, 90
Uris, Leon, 79

Weizmann, Chaim, 54
Wissenschaft des Judentums, 75
World Council of Synagogues,
  129

World Union for Progressive
  Judaism, 129

Yohanan ben Zakkai, R., 8

Zionism, Zionists, *passim*

DATE DUE
